Becoming a Strategic Business Owner

THE **GROWTH COACH**®

Driving Success. Balancing Life.[SM]

Becoming a Strategic Business Owner

A Proven Process to Enhance Your Strategic Mindset

Daniel M. Murphy

Library of Congress Control Number: 2004108585

Murphy, Daniel M.
Becoming a Strategic Business Owner: A Proven Process to Enhance Your Strategic Mindset

1. Marketing-Management
2. Strategic Planning
3. Success in Business

ISBN 0-9754456-0-X

The Growth Coach
Mailing Address: 10700 Montgomery Rd., Suite 300, Cincinnati, OH 45242
Telephone: 513-563-0570
www.TheGrowthCoach.com

Dedication

To the millions of small business owners, franchisees and self-employed professionals throughout North America desiring greater financial success, freedom and fun. With the right change in mindset and actions, you no longer have to endure feeling overworked, overwhelmed, frustrated or like a prisoner to your business.

Foreword

This book is in your hands because you want to get more out of your business and life. You are searching in the right resource. This practical book is intended to help drive the success and balance the lives of small business owners, franchisees, managers, and the self-employed. This resource will help you take your business to a higher level.

This book is also for the person who feels overworked, overwhelmed and like a prisoner to his or her business. It's for the owner experiencing more frustration than fun, more isolation than satisfaction. If you are overly busy and tired, this book will help you to slow down, reflect, face reality and decide on the critical changes you need to make to improve your business and personal life.

The good news is that you can achieve greater freedom, fulfillment, financial success and peace-of-mind. However, for your business and personal life to change, **you must change!** It will require you to think differently and act differently. To re-examine your role, your business, and your current life. To fall in love with your business again, **you** will have to adopt a strategic mindset, focus and approach to running your company. This book has the proven process to help.

INTRODUCTION

Men are not prisoners of fate, but only prisoners of their own minds. – Franklin D. Roosevelt

To begin, let me ask you some revealing questions. As a business owner, can you walk away from your business today for one or two months and come back to find it operating smoothly and profitably? Can you even escape for two weeks? Have you ever had a work-free vacation? If your answers are "no", you don't have a successful business, you have a glorified job in which you are trapped! You don't have an effective business system; you are the business system! You are a prisoner of your own making.

Let me be very clear. No matter what industry you are in, you should not be a prisoner to your business! If you are, you have it backwards. Your business should serve you and your dreams. It should give you greater freedom, not less. In fact, your business, properly designed, should function practically without you, not because of you. It should run predictably and automatically whether you are in the office or not, in the store or not, out in the field or not, on vacation or not. Your business should not depend upon your presence, personality, problem solving and perspiration for its daily survival. If so, your business does not work, you do!

Bottom line, you should run your business; it should not run you, your family or your life. Your business should work harder so you don't have to. It should be systems-dependent and not owner-dependent for its success. It should have its own heart, mind, and soul – it should not steal your vital organs and spirit!

Stop for a moment and think of the consequences. If everything in your business flows through you and is dependent upon you, then **you** are dramatically restricting the growth and profits of your company. As a single human being, there are natural limits to the amount of work, transactions, problems, and decisions that can flow effectively through you in a given day. Stop being a bottleneck or clog. Otherwise, you will continue to restrict the potential of your employees and business and ensure your persistent exhaustion. Stop missing out on greater personal freedom, money and happiness.

If you are the owner of a business (beyond the start-up phase) with annual revenue between $50,000 and $20 million, this book could be for you. If at times you feel like a prisoner or slave to your business or struggle to manage its growing size and complexity, this book is probably for you. If you wish to be more effective, work less and make more money, this book is definitely for you.

Furthermore, this book should be mandatory for any of your current or future advisers and coaches. These professionals can't help you if they don't understand your real issues, challenges and the strategic solutions that are available. Small business coaches affiliated with The Growth Coach® have been professionally trained and certified in our on-going coaching and accountability process and understand deeply the strategic solutions addressed briefly in this book.

On the flip side, this book is not intended for know-it-all entrepreneurs with a business still in diapers – at the start-up phase. No disrespect, but such proud owners are still blissfully naïve and high on the passion, promises and adrenaline rush associated with a newborn enterprise. They generally are too busy to hear this message. Starting out, such owners are willing to accept 12-hour workdays, being chained to the business, and intoxicated by the busyness and details of a new venture. However, the few wise enough to shape their businesses while still in the nursery will avoid many "growing pains" and headaches down the road. The sooner you adopt a strategic mindset, the better.

Think of this metaphor. Creating a baby is rather easy and enjoyable; raising a child is much more challenging. Similarly, starting a business is fairly simple and fun; managing a growing and complex business is much more difficult. As such, this book is aimed at the entrepreneur who faces the daily realities and challenges of managing a growing and chaotic business. The owner who is overwhelmed, overworked and wondering what the heck they got themselves into.

This book is for the owner who feels like a hostage to the business. It is for the owner who still feels compelled to control and do everything in the business. It is for the owner starting to question and re-examine his/her life, priorities and personal sacrifices. In short, this resource is intended to serve as a formula for freedom for any distraught entrepreneur who feels enslaved and overwhelmed by his or her business.

If you are seeking better approaches to managing your business and life, I can help. As an entrepreneur and business adviser/coach for over twenty years, I fully understand the unique mixture of pleasure and pain that comes with owning and managing a growing business. I have successfully founded a national franchise system of business coaches called, The Growth Coach®. I know the long hours and stress, the heavy burden of responsibilities, and the loneliness, fears and frustrations. I have spent my life helping small business owners, my heroes, to shape better businesses and shape better personal lives. If you are willing to keep an open mind, I am ready to help you. So are my certified coaches.

Let me be very clear, you are the expert in your business and industry. I am not and will never claim to be. My expertise is guiding business owners to unlock greater potential in themselves and their businesses. To help them enhance their strategic mindset, focus, actions and results. Over a decade ago, I developed a process to do just that called The Strategic Mindset ® Process.

This quarterly strategic-focusing process helps owners, like you, to slow down, reflect, and decide on the critical changes necessary to improve their businesses and personal lives. They discover practical and highly effective personal management and business management strategies and mindsets. They gain clarity of direction, peace-of-mind and greater confidence pursuing their business and personal goals. This year-round coaching and accountability process has become the foundation for The Growth Coach®, a national company specializing in coaching small businesses.

Through this book and the strategic path I map out, I guide owners to become more effective, focused and productive. The life-changing process described within this book allows owners to go to work "on" their businesses, "on" themselves, and "on" their specific issues, opportunities and goals.

This book, this process, helps owners to face reality – to see what is working and what is not working in their lives and businesses. It helps them to "burn off the fog" that keeps them from seeing their businesses and personal lives for what they really are – not as they wish, hope or dream them to be.

This book shows you how to remove the clutter and non-essential "stuff" from your days. To prevent you from wasting your time, talents and life-force on the wrong activities – the trivial many. Rather, this book helps you to identify the highest and best use of your time and talents – getting you focused on the vital few activities that produce massive results.

This resource should help you to better learn about yourself and what you truly desire from life and your business. After all, knowing who you are, what you want and where you are going creates a powerful sense of clarity. Few owners possess such clarity and confidence.

For the last thirteen years in particular, I have been on a crusade to re-educate and re-focus business owners to lead more, work less, and enjoy greater freedom, financial success and happiness. In short, trying to get owners to think and act strategically and effectively.

Are you a strategic business owner? To find out, ask yourself the following questions:

- Do you see the big picture and have a long-term view?
- Do you think more like a CEO than an employee?
- Do you create an annual business plan?
- Is your leadership purposeful, proactive, and planning-based?
- Do you constantly think about the direction and objectives of the business?
- Do you focus on your entire business and not just the technical work of your business?
- Have you created plans, procedures and policies to help operate your company?
- Have you developed and documented all your key business processes?
- Do you utilize the leverage of marketing to grow your business?
- Do you spend more time on important matters rather than trivial/urgent matters?
- Have you created a systems-dependent business instead of an owner-dependent business?
- Do you conduct one-on-one monthly coaching sessions with your managers and/or key employees?
- Do you avoid getting buried in the day-to-day details and headaches of the business?
- Have you shaped your business more by design than by default?
- Are you experiencing more fun and fulfillment than frustrations?

If you answered "no" to most of these questions, you can benefit greatly from this book on becoming a strategic business owner. In short, a strategic business owner (SBO) gets the highest and best return possible for his time, money and effort. He or she focuses on working smarter, not harder. So does this book.

Be warned however, this book is not an easy read. I don't write in entertaining fables or parables. That's not my style and that's not how I have helped hundreds of business owners over the years get free from the debilitating details of their companies. If you want entertainment, buy a novel or watch HBO. This book contains real world, in-your-face, practical advice. While this medicine may not always taste great, this prescription should help you feel better about yourself, your business, and your life.

If you want different results, you must take different steps. You must get out of your comfort zone, stop the excuses, face reality and acknowledge something is broken. Turn down the ego. It is time to become honest, time to reflect, and time to re-focus. It's time to stop treating the symptoms and start addressing the real points of pain. Be prepared to re-think, re-calibrate and re-organize your business and management approach to achieve long-term solutions to your hassles and headaches.

Regardless of how frazzled and swamped you may feel, know that there is hope for real relief. Your past does not have to equal your future. Whether you have no employees, 10 employees, 100 or 1,000 employees, there are practical solutions to gain more freedom, flexibility, and fulfillment in your life. **However, the answer is not to shift into higher gear; it is to shift mindsets. For you workaholics, let me repeat. Sustained relief comes from shifting mindsets and strategies, not gears. You must adopt a strategic mindset.** To gain a fresh start, you will need to re-boot your mental software and try new attitudes and strategic approaches.

At my very core, I am a teacher. I have gained invaluable insights and lessons to share with you as a business owner myself and as a marketing consultant, a strategic planning facilitator, a business coach, a sales/marketing executive, a sales trainer, and a CPA. From these experiences, I feel well qualified to help business owners to get strategic, get free, and get happy.

This resource will help you transform your mind and habits in order to transform your business and life for the better. This educational journey will allow you to re-design your business and re-gain your personal life and freedom. While I can't promise you nirvana, I am confident this book will help you map out your path to guilt-free liberation. It will connect the dots to reveal a more enjoyable and less stressful way to run your business and life. It will help you shape your business by design, not by default.

Henry David Thoreau stated, "Things do not change; we change." I hope to share valuable lessons and insights with you that will help you change and rediscover the joy, passion and blessings of being a business owner.

Daniel M. Murphy

"Enhancing the strategic mindset, focus and results of small business owners, franchisees, managers, and the self-employed."

TABLE OF CONTENTS

Face Reality

Points to Ponder

- *We are slaves to whatever we don't understand.*
  Vernon Howard
- *Honesty is the first chapter of the book of wisdom.*
  Thomas Jefferson
- *Nothing about ourselves can be changed until it is first accepted.*
  Sheldon Kopp
- *We lie loudest when we lie to ourselves.*
  Eric Hoffer
- *The first and best victory is to conquer self.*
  Plato

Entrepreneurial Reflection

Not everything that is faced can be changed, but nothing can be changed until it is faced.

For many of you, in as little as two to three years (and regardless of the level of financial success achieved), your entrepreneurial dream of freedom, independence and wealth has started to warp into a partial nightmare. Your wish to be master of your destiny has degenerated into your being a slave to your business, your employees and your customers. The fire in your belly has been replaced by a growing uneasiness in your gut.

Habitually, you are still working too many hours, wearing too many hats, and handling too many things. Sadly, the entrepreneurial lows have become deeper, last longer and are more frequent. As your business has grown, your fun and fulfillment have not. In fact, most of you suffer from the generalized feelings of anxiety, mental fatigue, and of being trapped in the business. For sake of simplicity, I have termed these feelings, **the business owner blues.**

For years, you have deluded yourself. You kept telling yourself that one day you would get caught up, slow down, and have more free time to do other things. That the blues would eventually fade. In reality, the sixty to seventy hour workweeks continue. The stress continues. You can't even escape the business for a few relaxing, no-work days. You still scramble like a hyperactive squirrel preparing for a harsh winter.

Furthermore, you are coming to realize that being a workaholic, micro-manager, control freak, dictator or hands-on technician does not work and is a miserable way to run a business, much less lead a life. Working harder, acting tougher, or being more involved with daily details is not the path to greater freedom, joy, or peace-of-mind. Rather, it is a guaranteed path to burn out.

How did you get to this point? Odds are, you were a gifted technician (programmer, electrician, painter, landscaper, CPA, mechanic, chef, attorney, carpenter, salesperson, etc.) who caught the "entrepreneurial bug" several years ago and started, acquired or inherited a business – one that probably mirrors your technical skills and experience. Now, as you try frantically to maintain control of your growing company, you are likely overworked, overwhelmed and suffering from a full-blown case of the business owner blues. You are tired. You feel like a slave to your business. As it grows, you work harder and become deeper enslaved. The work, the problems, and the company revolve around you.

If you are honest, business ownership is probably quite different from what you expected and from what you have been prepared to handle. If not held in check, the very strengths that made you a successful technician (detail orientation, hands-on doer, technical expertise, day-to-day focus, etc.) can be real liabilities to you as a business owner.

Technical expertise alone is never sufficient to build and manage a healthy and profitable business. You must provide the vision and leadership of a Chief Executive Officer (CEO) and the order and systems of a Manager. You must get strategic to get free! You must learn to focus on the entire business, not merely the technical work of the business. You must elevate your mindset, focus and actions – focusing on the vital few things that really matter and make a difference.

For example, being a good plumber contrasted with creating and operating a successful plumbing business are two different worlds and sets of challenges. Each role requires very different mindsets and skillsets. To be effective, the latter requires strategic leadership; the former requires technical "doer-ship". Just because you know how to do the daily technical work of plumbing doesn't qualify you to design, build and manage a business that does the work of plumbing. This is a fatal assumption most would-be entrepreneurs make.

If you are a technician masquerading as an owner, be warned! Your pipes may burst. You have the wrong perspective and are doing the wrong type of work. Because you are comfortable with and good at doing the technical work (for example, plumbing), by default and out of habit, as your company grows, you will end up doing more and more plumbing work. You will find it hard to escape the frantic pace. Soon, the business will have you and your life held hostage. You will forever be trapped under the sink or hovering over a broken toilet. Why? Because your business is broken too! You are not thinking and functioning as a strategic business owner; you are toiling and sweating like a plumber.

Time to Face Facts

Accept the fact that it is no accident you hold this book in your hands. Out of either inspiration or desperation, you are seeking alternative approaches. Your current beliefs, habits and actions are not yielding the results you want. Odds are, you desire greater success, peace-of-mind and joy. I too want you to achieve greater pleasure from your business. Furthermore, in addition to your business plan, I want you to have a fulfilling life plan. I want you to make a life that works for you, not just make a living from your work. I want you to be successful **and** happy. I want to help drive your success and balance your life!

For change to occur, however, you must stop playing mind games and admit that something about your business is not working. While sacrificing long hours each week may have been necessary the first few years, continuation of such a frantic pace is symptomatic of deeper issues. You should not live this way! Something is wrong. Something is off. You know it in your gut. Others probably sense it in your moods, in your eyes and on your face.

It is time to face reality! You and your business have some problems that require some solutions. Very simply, you can't change what you do not openly acknowledge. A problem properly identified and acknowledged is a problem half solved.

To begin the transformation and healing process, you need to do some serious reflection. Be brutally honest when you answer these questions:

- Do I often question, "Why do I have to do every darn thing myself?"
- Am I still working too much and making too little?
- Am I trapped working "in" my business instead of "on" my business?

- Do I ever wonder if business ownership is truly worth the time, effort, headaches, hassles, and sacrifices?
- Do I feel trapped on a treadmill, moving faster and faster, but going nowhere?
- Do I constantly face frequent interruptions and repetitive questions from my staff?
- Do I go home many nights feeling mentally and physically drained?
- Do I confuse busyness with accomplishment?
- Do I dread the drudgery of facing and solving the same issues and problems each and every day – the burden of re-creating the wheel time and time again?
- Do I daydream about regaining my sense of freedom, joy, passion, and peace-of-mind?
- Do I have anxiety about drowning in projects, problems, deadlines, crises, meetings, employee issues, unanswered voicemails/emails, customer complaints, administrative trivia, and on and on?
- Do I feel like a master juggler with too many balls up in the air and dreading they will soon begin hitting the floor?
- Am I forever chained to a phone, computer, email, or pager?
- Am I tired of having customers rely on me personally for services, solutions and satisfaction?
- Am I fed up with missing family time, family events, and making other personal sacrifices on a semi-regular basis?
- Do I crave more free time to do the things that matter most to me?

Admit to the Problem

If you answered "yes" to most of these questions, don't feel guilty, ashamed or embarrassed. You are not alone. Most owners have never learned to be strategic. Role models are scarce. As such, dysfunctional businesses and owners are the rule, not the exception.

Like you, most owners feel that they have been sentenced to a life of servitude and some even suffer from the blues. Unfortunately, because of pride, shame or ignorance, this sad condition has been kept hidden in the corner office for too long. Through this book, it is time to unveil this entrepreneurial, dirty secret.

Starting now, you should not have to endure this much discomfort and frustration associated with your business. You do not have to live this way! You should not be consumed by your business and frustrated with your life. Stop and think, why in the world, as the owner, should you have to touch every transaction, be involved with every decision, help solve every problem, or handle everybody's job in some fashion? You shouldn't! It doesn't make sense. Something is broken! You cannot succeed alone. You don't have enough hours in a day or enough energy or bandwidth to go it alone. Pain is a good indication that something is damaged and needs to be healed!

Let this book serve as your shock therapy. Realize that you aren't the only one suffering. Think about how your stress and blues are negatively impacting your employees, customers, vendors/suppliers, friends and if applicable, your spouse and kids. Hear this wake-up call! It is time to radically shift your business beliefs and behavior. It is time to expand your view of new possibilities for managing your business and life. The better your business functions, the better your life will function.

You deserve to be free from the daily grind; after all, you own a business, not a job. You should actually enjoy the journey of developing and running a business and not defer your personal life and happiness until you retire or sell. Live life now! Do not get so caught up in making a living that you forget to make a life. If your personal life is suffering because of your company, either your leadership approach is misguided or your business design is broken, maybe both!

At this point, simply admit that your business centers on you and is totally dependent upon you. Admit that you are buried up to your eyeballs in the details of the business. Admit that you are a prisoner to your business. Admit that instead of your business giving you greater life, it continues to drain more of your personal time and peace-of-mind. Admit that while your headaches and hassles grow, your freedom shrinks.

As you will see, most, if not all of these problems center on your being a day-to-day focused owner instead of a strategic business owner. To get free, you will have to get strategic. You need to adopt a strategic mindset, focus and approach to running your business and your life.

Get a Coach

The famous psychologist, Abraham Maslow, has stated, "What is necessary to change a person is to change his awareness of himself." After serving entrepreneurs over many years, I have learned that you will not make the changes necessary to improve your life and business without someone holding your feet to the fire. You could benefit from a business coach or better yet, a year-round coaching and accountability process. You need someone observing the truth, that is, your outward and repeated behavior. Human nature doesn't allow for such objective self-evaluation and feedback. Humans are too subjective. We judge our surroundings and ourselves by our inward perceptions of reality, which very often are mild distortions if not complete illusions.

Even with this guidebook, you will not be able to achieve such a strategic transformation on your own. No significant and sustainable changes will occur without a real-world evaluation and accountability process. You will need additional coaching to achieve real and lasting breakthroughs. Even great athletes (i.e. Tiger Woods) need coaches to help elevate their thinking, talents and results.

You will need an objective, caring coach who will challenge you and hold you accountable for growing and changing. Someone who helps burn off the mental fog that is clouding your objectivity. Someone to challenge your old, limiting assumptions. Someone who monitors your progress. Someone who holds you to a higher standard of success and excellence. Someone to ask you the tough questions. Someone to get you to slow down and do deep reflection and analysis. Someone who helps you define and achieve both your personal and business goals.

You will need an objective coach that can help you re-think and re-calibrate your assumptions and approaches. A professional business coach will help you achieve this critical renewal of the mind. You must move away from typical business owner practices and beliefs. Conformity is your jailer. For maximum results, engage a dedicated business coach – someone who has a proven process to help you get more of what you want and less of what you don't.

To work with someone who knows the philosophy and methodology of this book inside and out, search out a small business coach affiliated with The Growth Coach®. They are professionally trained and certified in The Strategic Mindset® Process, our year-round coaching and accountability process. The quarterly strategic-focusing process is affordable, guaranteed, and will help you make the necessary transformations of mindset, habits and business strategies.

Regardless of the help you choose, be open and be coachable. Meet regularly with your coach. For some, quarterly is enough. For others, monthly coaching is necessary. Ask him or her to monitor your adopting and implementing the philosophies, strategies and habits as suggested in this book. The value of receiving candid, objective feedback on your progress during these accountability sessions cannot be overstated.

Other Tips & Suggestions

As you will discover, the success system in your hands is a practical and no-nonsense guidebook that comes from the collective success, pain and lessons of others. The wisdom captured here emanates from my own business successes and failures along with the struggles and triumphs of the many clients I have served over the years.

Please realize, however, there are no shortcuts or tricks contained in this book. You, and you alone, are the agent of change. You must tame your mind so that it doesn't automatically react in old, harmful, habitual ways. You must internalize and fully apply these ideas in a way that is unique to, and appropriate for, you and your business. Adopt and adapt.

Guard against dismissing these ideas as simple and obvious. As most things in life, success is less about ideas and more about aggressive implementation. Knowing what to do and doing what you know are very different things. Your task is to consider carefully these ideas and then fully implement those that make sense for your business. Again, use your accountability coach to get important things done!

For self-employed owners (soloists), you should begin to apply these strategies as you grow your business and add employees. Your challenge will be to define and document the different job functions you currently perform and eventually hire people to replace you in those technical roles. Even if you decide to remain solo, you can still benefit greatly from the strategic discussions on a CEO mindset, business system creation and documentation, leadership, business planning, marketing, people management, and learning to let go.

As you will undoubtedly note, certain themes and ideas will repeat throughout the book. This is not a case of redundancy but a belief in the power of repetition. Some new ideas need to be sown continually to take root. Studies show it takes three exposures to a new idea before it is learned, a fourth exposure to reinforce it, and a fifth to internalize it and own it. Embrace the repetition and don't fight it.

Make this book your own. Highlight key ideas and jot down key thoughts. Only when an idea is written down do you truly own it. Make good ideas your prisoners. Write down those philosophies and strategies that you wish to implement.

Finally, judge this book on its effectiveness of transforming your mind from doer to leader and from that of an employee to that of a CEO. If this book helps transform you to be more strategic and proactive, you will be well on your way to more profits, more joy, more freedom and more peace-of-mind.

However, don't be unrealistic or impatient with your transformation. You won't change your mindset overnight. Stepping out of your comfort zone will take on-going courage. You may take a step back to advance two steps ahead. It will take some time and help from your coach or a coaching process; don't get discouraged. The long-term joy will be worth the short-term discomfort and sacrifice.

The answers and wisdom you seek are already within you; this book will merely help release them if you are ready. I pray that you have the humility to keep an open mind, the willingness to change your mindset, the courage to unlearn some of your assumptions, and the resolve to take aggressive action on some new ideas, philosophies, and strategies.

Suggested Action Items:

- Admit to yourself that something is broken in the way you have designed and lead your business. Resolve to take corrective action with the help from this book.
- If you have not done so, mark the heck out of this book – write down notes, highlight key concepts, etc. Go back and underline key revelations. Make this book your own.
- After reading each chapter, take aggressive action on Suggested Action Items appropriate to your situation. Jot down your own to-do list as well.
- Commit to finishing this book within 30 days. Share this pledge with a key person in your life. Give that person a firm date 30 days out by which you will be finished. In 15 days, have him or her contact you in order to gauge your progress. Encourage them to kick your butt if necessary.
- Insist that each of your key business advisers reads this book as well to foster a common understanding and vocabulary of the process needed to improve your business and your personal life. If they aren't willing to partner with you in this important journey, consider getting new advisers!
- As most things in life, success is less about ideas and more about aggressive implementation. Knowing what to do and doing what you know are very different things. Select an accountability coach within the next 21 days. Choose someone you trust to hold you accountable for objectively reviewing your business and personal life and for making the changes necessary to improve your freedom, joy, and profits. Most important, have them help you to adopt a strategic

mindset. Ideally, you want a business coach with a proven, year-round coaching/accountability process.

- Accept fully that you, and you alone, are the agent of change. Take full responsibility for your transformation.
- After you have thoroughly read this book, start meeting with your coach on a regular basis (quarterly or monthly). In your one-on-one coaching sessions, you may wish to focus on each chapter of this guidebook.
- Buy a copy of this book for your coach and insist that your coach thoroughly reads and understands the strategies in this book. Your coach can't help you if she or he does not know the process.
- Embrace the power and benefits of repetition. Also, make good ideas your prisoners – write them down. Take voluminous notes and capture ideas in writing.

Your Path to Greater Freedom & Fortune – A Quick Overview

Points to Ponder

- *Don't forget until too late that the business of life is not business, but living.*

  B.C. Forbes
- *If you keep doing what you've always done, you'll keep getting what you've always got.*

  Peter Francisco
- *It's not what you don't know that hurts you; it's what you know that ain't so.*

  Mark Twain
- *For things to change, you've got to change. Otherwise, not much will change.*

  Jim Rohn
- *It is not enough to be busy; so are the ants. The question is: What are we busy about?*

  Henry David Thoreau

Congratulations. You have admitted that you are a prisoner to your business and need to get free from the tyranny of the daily grind and the nauseating details. Because you are still reading, I assume you are committed to escaping your reactive world and entering the purposeful, proactive and planning-based world of the strategic business owner. That's terrific. You are on your path to recovery and to greater freedom.

What Leads to Business Imprisonment?

Before we start solving some of your issues, we need to examine the basic causes of business owner bondage. What are the common traps? How do the chains get tighter and tighter?

Specifically, I consider the following five to be the most common traps for business owner bondage: (1) technical tendencies, (2) busyness (3) ineffective leadership and delegation, (4) inadequate or missing business systems, and (5) growing business complexities.

1) Technical Tendencies:

Habits determine destiny. Too many entrepreneurs are former technicians now masquerading as owners. They think they are entrepreneurs, but they don't act that way. As once accomplished technicians, they have a hard time letting go of such expertise and familiarity. They remain trapped in a technical comfort zone, mindset and work approach. Sadly, such technical expertise is insufficient for managing a business. Moreover, they fail to develop the visionary, strategic, and leadership skills necessary to run a successful business.

2) Busyness:

Many owners confuse activity with accomplishment. They confuse busyness with results. Hard work with smart work. Perspiration with purpose. Efficiency (doing things right) with effectiveness (doing the right things). Instead of working smarter, many owners hold tight to the delusion that working harder and harder is the solution. They keep trying to shift into higher and higher gears. The more the business grows, the harder they work, the more imprisoned they become. No matter how much energy you expend, however, wrong strategies inevitably lead to poor results – less freedom and more headaches. It is like trying to catch fish in a pond with your bare hands. No matter how many hours you work or how deep you wade, a poor strategy leads to poor results – no fish dinner!

3) Ineffective Leadership & Delegation
Far too many small business owners are by default small leaders. This costs them dearly. Instead of leadership, they excel at doer-ship. They are micro-managers that like to touch and control everything. They trust no one but themselves. They believe "no one does it as well as me." They seldom delegate, if at all. They mistake such busyness for business leadership. Instead of thinking and leading like owners, most think and behave like employees. Instead of reflecting and planning, they excel at sweating and doing. They act like they have a job instead of owning a business.

4) Inadequate Business Systems
A vast majority of owners don't know how to design a new business or re-engineer an existing one to be more systems-oriented and professionally equipped with plans, procedures and policies. As a result, entrepreneurs don't create and document the processes (specific and repeatable ways to do something), procedures and policies that allow for well organized, smoothly running, easier-to-manage companies. Without defining and documenting the specific work that needs to be done, owners can't delegate effectively and eventually remove themselves from their technical roles. As a result, owners are forever feeling out of control. Tragically, most entrepreneurs have unknowingly, reactively and accidentally created an

owner-centered and owner-dependent company. They are trapped!

5) Growing Business Complexities:

A growing business with its increasing number of customers, transactions and problems will eventually crush a business not properly designed and prepared to handle such growth. Without effective leadership and adequate business systems (an integrated web of processes), a growing company does not stand a chance. Growing pains are unavoidable. Producing predictable and consistent results will be nearly impossible. By failing to plan for growth, you are by default planning to fail.

Technical bias, busyness, poor delegation, inadequate leadership and business systems, and the growing complexities of a business lead to a life sentence of working on the chain gang – your company. Fortunately, this book, along with your willingness to change, can serve as your *get out of jail free card*. It will help you to escape the blues and the tyranny of technical busyness. You will no longer have to be the jack-of-all-trades for your company. Growing pains will subside. You will learn to be master, not servant. You will learn to lead more and work less. You will learn to shape your company by design, not by default.

The Freedom & Fortune Trail for Owners

After interacting with several hundred entrepreneurs from all types of industries since 1985, I have learned with absolute clarity that your goal as a business owner should be to design a company that is distinct from you and quite candidly, works in your absence. You should create a separate cash flow entity, not merely a job for yourself. It should pay you a healthy salary plus a return on your investment of money, time and effort. You should build equity! You should build wealth! Bottom line, your role should be to shape, manage and grow this independent and enduring asset – your business.

Your enterprise should function without you, not because of you. I know this sounds bizarre, but hear me out. While you can be the brains behind the enterprise, you should not be like Hercules trying to hold up the entire weight of the company! You will be crushed!

Your business should work harder so you don't have to. You should be able to make money everyday without having to work everyday. You should invest more brain equity and leadership equity and much less sweat equity into your company. Your business should be a product of your brain, not your brawn.

You should strive to build a business that does not enslave you and does not rely on your being present every minute of every day doing all the thinking, deciding, worrying, and working. You must adopt a new way of thinking and acting.

You must become a strategic business owner. Specifically, you must learn to adopt a CEO mindset; systematize and document your business; lead more and work less; create a simple business plan; utilize the leverage of marketing; effectively manage your greatest asset, your people; and learn to let go. In short, you must transform the way you see yourself and your business.

As a strategic business owner, your primary aim should be to develop a self-managing and systems-oriented business that runs consistently, predictably, smoothly, and profitably while you are not there. You should shape and own the business system (again, an integrated web of processes) and employ competent and caring employees to operate the system. You should document the work of your business so that you can effectively train others to execute the work. You must make yourself replaceable in the technical trenches of your business. To repeat, define and document the specific work to be done and then train and delegate. This is how you begin successfully to beat the blues, escape death by details, and gain greater freedom.

With a documented operating system, your employees should be able to carry on the work of the business while you focus on big picture priorities or for heaven's sake, decide to take a break. You should be able to escape the daily drudgery. In fact, your company should run on autopilot status even while you're on an extended, work-free, guilt-free vacation. If it does, you will have designed and built a business that truly works and is worth a fortune. More importantly, in the process, you will have gained back a personal life that is fulfilling.

To maintain freedom, independence and fulfillment as your business grows, so must your leadership effectiveness and operating systems. You must stop micro-managing and start leading (macro-managing). You must become more purposeful and proactive. This guidebook will help you become a strategic business owner by addressing seven critical steps:

1) **Step One:** Learn to work **on** yourself by transitioning to a new way of thinking and behaving. Re-program yourself and your habits. Stop acting like an employee and start thinking

like a CEO. Learn to work **on** your business, not **in** your business. Adopt the theory of optimization. Be strategic, not tactical; work less, lead more!

2) **Step Two:** Systematize your company by creating, documenting and continually improving all your key processes, procedures and policies. Trust the business system and personnel you put in place and remove yourself from the company's daily details. Be more hands-off and more brains-on. Replace yourself with other people. Define and document the work to be done. Train others and delegate the work. This operating system is your foundation for freedom.

3) **Step Three:** Increase your leadership capabilities. Excel at leadership, not doer-ship. Your business needs a clear vision and strong leader to hold others accountable, not another employee doing technical work. Help build and direct your team.

4) **Step Four:** Develop clarity of direction for your business and employees by creating a simple business plan and an effective implementation process.

5) **Step Five:** Learn to effectively manage your people, your greatest asset.

6) **Step Six:** Instead of incremental growth, engage the leverage of marketing to achieve substantial, profitable growth.

7) **Step Seven:** Learn to let go, delegate, and truly enjoy business ownership, your relationships, and your life.

By working less **in** your business, you gain more time to work **on** your business and make those essential changes necessary to optimize your company and your life. This seven-step approach is the path to eliminating the blues and ownership bondage and re-acquiring the fire for your business and life! Again, it's your formula to greater freedom, fulfillment and fortunes.

You may well be skeptical. That's normal. However, let me ask you, "Are your current paths and strategies working?" If so, you wouldn't be searching for answers here. If not, I invite you to acknowledge the problems in your business, take responsibility for them, and dare to try new approaches.

Suggested Action Items:

- Review the five traps of business bondage and identify which ones are your personal challenges. Shares these issues with your coach.
- Re-read the seven-step strategic business owner process beginning on page 18 to achieve greater freedom, financial success and happiness. Understand where the book is going and why you should commit to invest time and energy in this educational journey.
- Pledge to re-design your business so that you are not at the heart of every transaction, problem, decision, etc.
- Checking up on prior commitments, have you already:
  - Selected a coach to help transform you into a Strategic Business Owner (SBO)?
  - Committed to reading this book in 30 days?
  - Scheduled out your regular coaching sessions?
  - Asked your loved ones and key advisers to read this book?
  - Taken notes, highlighted key concepts?

SHIFTING FROM AN EMPLOYEE TO A CEO MINDSET

Points to Ponder

- *The significant problems we face cannot be solved at the level of thinking that created them.*

  Albert Einstein

- *If everything is important, then nothing is.*

  Unknown

- *The difficulty lies not so much in developing new ideas as in escaping from old ones.*

  John Maynard Keynes

- *You are searching for the magic key that will unlock the door to the source of power; and yet you have the key in your own hands, and you may use it the moment you learn to control your thoughts.*

  Napoleon Hill

- *It's what you learn after you know it all that counts.*

  John Wooden

- *Wealth is the product of man's capacity to think.*

  Ayn Rand

It's All in Your Mind

Through this book, I will hold up a merciless mirror to your face that will force you to examine cause-and-effect relationships – how your current beliefs, strategies and actions are causing your frustrations and loss of freedom. Please slow down, reflect deeply and adopt a new way of seeing your business and yourself as its leader. Hopefully, you will come to the conclusion that you must change your mindset, leadership approach and business strategies as suggested in this book to achieve a more fulfilling and financially rewarding life.

Education literally means, "to change within". Please be open to let this book educate you and change you, especially some of your business assumptions and beliefs. All meaningful progress is the result of change. By changing your mindset and habits (repeated behavior), you change your life.

Since 1985, much of my mission has centered on healing the hearts, minds, and souls of beleaguered business owners. These entrepreneurs needed rescuing, not from their competition, but from their own limiting mindsets, flawed assumptions, and self-sabotaging habits. More important than helping to re-engineer their businesses, I help owners to re-engineer their minds and attitudes.

Put simply, I coach entrepreneurs to conquer themselves first, the marketplace second. I get owners to re-think and re-focus their approaches. I help them to work more **on** themselves and **on** their businesses and less **in** their businesses. By working less in the daily details, these owners are freed up to transform their lives and businesses for the better.

Be a CEO, not an Employee

Worth repeating, before you can fully re-engineer your business, you must first re-engineer your mindset. You need to tame and calm your mind to free it from reactive, counterproductive habits. You must adopt a strategic mindset and focus.

Please adopt this simple change management formula -- **BE-DO-HAVE**. In order to **have**, you must **do**, and in order to **do** effectively, you must truly **be**. For example, want to **have** a better golf handicap? Then you must **do** certain things: take lessons, practice and play more, get better clubs, etc. However, all this doing won't be optimally effective unless you first change your mindset – you must **be** a better golfer on the inside. You must start to see, feel, think and behave like a better golfer in order to be a better golfer.

Similarly, in order to **have** more freedom, joy and financial success as an owner, you must **do** new strategies (i.e. systematize your business, utilize marketing, etc.). In order to optimally do these strategies, you must first **be** a more effective business owner – mind, body and soul. Like an award-winning actor, do not just play the part, become the part. You must change on the inside before your external realities change.

How do you escape the nauseating details and headaches of your business? How do you gain greater freedom? You must make the great mental leap from that of employee to that of a business leader. First, you must acknowledge your technical bias, your addiction to being busy, and your uneasiness with delegation. Next you must adopt the "big picture" mindset of a Chief Executive Officer (CEO). You must **be** a CEO in mind and spirit to get the results you seek. You must think, feel, see, taste, smell and hear like a CEO. This chapter will help you out.

If you don't start thinking like a CEO, it will be nearly impossible for you to start behaving like a strategic business owner and truly working **on** your business in a proactive, purposeful manner. For many owners, jumping this wide chasm from employee to owner is tough and terrifying. However, you will never escape a workaholic existence unless you stop being a detailed-oriented technician masquerading as an owner. Stop focusing on the technical work of the business; focus on the entire business. The choice is yours. Step up and be a leader, not a micro-manager!

The Technician's Addiction

Instead of working **on** their businesses, most owners are trapped working **in** their businesses, slaving away and grinding it out. Instead of working on tomorrow, they are preoccupied with working in today. They end up majoring in minor things. They worry about office supplies instead of office processes. They focus on accounting details instead of holding their employees accountable. They worry about the company's vision plan instead of planning the company's vision. They react with short-term, short-lived fixes instead of proactively creating long-term solutions. They fixate on their mail, email, or cell phone calls instead of communicating their expectations to their key managers or employees. They obsess with doing things right instead of doing the right things. They do the wrong type of work really well. They are chasing their tails!

Are you trapped in the body and mind of a doer instead of a leader? Be honest, do you fall into the routine of doing the work of an employee or technician instead of the work of an owner or leader? Do you neglect such areas as vision creation, strategic planning, establishing priorities and goals, organizational design, business system development, profit improvement, team development, employee accountability, etc?

As previously discussed, you were probably a successful technician that caught the entrepreneurial bug several years ago and bought, inherited or started a business related to your technical skills. You are too comfortable with and good at handling such details. Such expertise, unfortunately, has a strong tendency to suck you into the nooks and crannies of the business. For you, the technical day-to-day guts of the business are addictive and tough to escape. Sadly, a technician's mindset and mode of operation are insufficient for running a business. These technical assets can be real liabilities and traps for an owner trying to be more proactive and strategic.

For example, maybe you were a gifted house painter who thought, "I can start a painting business on my own." From the get go, you probably functioned in a technical capacity and never grew your leadership capacity or the business systems. You worried about selling and performing painting jobs. You probably didn't worry about how to design and build a painting business with you as CEO. Rather, you dove in, got busy-being-busy, and started functioning as a painter, chief salesperson, estimator, bookkeeper, materials supplier, quality control supervisor, etc.

Consequently, you function as a jack-of-all-trades painter that also happens to own a house painting company. You are more technician than leader. Instead of focusing on the business of painting, you focus on the technical work of painting. You probably spend far too much time painting or micro-managing your other painters and not enough time painting your company's future. Because of your technical comfort zone, you are trapped doing the work of a painter, not the strategic work of a leader.

Here are a few more examples to drive home the point. Being a good computer programmer and running a successful programming business are two different roles and worlds. Writing code is technical and tactical work. Just because you know how to do the daily technical work of programming, for example, doesn't mean you know how to design, build and manage a business that does the work of programming. Programming code has not prepared you for the key functions of a business -- selling, marketing, client service, finance, leadership, business systems, people management, etc. Technical experience is insufficient background for running a business.

Similarly, if your background is selling, finance or production, your bias will get you buried in the selling, financial and production details of the business. You must escape your technical conditioning! Hire others to handle such matters, if necessary.

Business ownership is all about strategic leadership, not technical doer-ship. Few owners understand and appreciate such critical distinctions. Tragically, owners mistake a technician's orientation for that of an entrepreneur's. They mistake busy-being-busy activity for accomplishment. They confuse hard work for intelligent work. They have a technician's addiction to detail work. Sadly, they work and think like employees instead of owners. They do the wrong type of work. They fail to grasp that running a business is strategic, entrepreneurial, visionary, and requires strong leadership.

Contributing Factors

If the technical background or DNA weren't enough of a challenge, lack of role models and faulty educations compound the problem of being addicted to technical busyness.

Let's face facts; there are too many technicians, workaholics, micro-managers and dictators in the small business world and not enough CEOs. Because of poor role models and faulty business educations, owners do not get to see fresh, successful alternatives.

Unfortunately, our business education system focuses too much on technical knowledge and not nearly enough on leadership development and organizational design. Instead of teaching an opportunity mindset, our education system focuses on everything that can go wrong. As such, we scare owners into the deadly mistake of thinking that "they must do everything themselves" to get it right.

As a result, owners fail to put proper systems and processes into place to help guide other employees and the business. Without systems to help them lead, owners end up micro-managing. They can't delegate effectively. Soon, the business outgrows their personal capabilities and time constraints. The dreaded growing pains follow because they failed to grow their leadership capabilities, business systems, and employees. They are trapped on the business owner treadmill, tackling non-strategic work, expending more and more energy, and going nowhere. No wonder they have the blues and no free time. Now, the owner is at risk of burning out and the business of crashing in.

Practical Strategies

Allow me to get in your face for a moment. You own a business, not a job! Wake up; you are the owner, not another employee! Most companies are over-managed and grossly under-led. Start leading! Start thinking and planning more and sweating less. Use more mind power, less muscle power. Every group craves an engaged and energetic leader to direct them toward a common cause and challenge them to greater heights. Be that person for your employees. While there can be many employees, there can be only one leader. You are it! Start filling the role.

Even if you are a solo practitioner, thinking like a CEO is a critical step as you grow and replace yourself in various technical roles with new employees. Even if you decide to go it alone, you will see that the CEO mindset will pay you great dividends as you better manage your time, resources and clients/customers.

As CEO, you need to work **on** the business: its purpose, direction, strategy, structure, systems, people, goals, and accountability processes. Again, see the whole business, not just its parts. Have an aerial view to know where you want to go and how you want to shape your business. Instead of shuffling papers or doing the bookkeeping, decide how to make your company different, better, more profitable and more systems-oriented. Think and act like a business architect. Again, your goal is to design and shape a business that serves you and works independently from you -- a business that is systems-dependent and not owner-dependent. You want a business that runs nearly on autopilot and spits out cash.

As a leader, you need to be more strategic, long-term focused and less tactical/technical, day-to-day fixated. If you don't focus on the entire business, no one else will. It will just drift or run aground. So how do you stop thinking and acting like an employee or technician? Here are nine steps to consider seriously:

1. First, you should change the metaphor in your head for what it means to be an owner. Regardless of your industry or size of your business, start viewing yourself as a CEO, not an employee. Instead of seeing yourself as a role player, see yourself as a head coach. Effective owners I know prefer to view themselves as a director, conductor, facilitator, or captain. Regardless, choose a metaphor for what it means to be a leader.

2. To help with this mindset transformation, start referring to yourself as CEO. Put it on your business card, stationery, etc. Using the term CEO will force you to see your company as an entity above and beyond yourself, as a separate and valuable asset that needs to be professionally managed and optimized. You are not the business and the business is not you. Spend time and energy helping to build, improve and optimize this asset. For example, focus on how to grow sales, expand your competitive advantage, and increase your value to customers.

3. Consider that as CEO, you get paid at least the equivalent of $200 an hour to professionally manage this separate entity and valuable asset – your business. Ask yourself before you touch any task, "Would a CEO do this?" Or ask, "Is this task worth me doing at a cost of $200 an hour?" Don't spend a dollar's worth of time on a dime decision or task. Elevate your vision, thinking and tasks.

4. If you truly buy into your role as a CEO, you should be willing to give up the urgent, less important, low-value tasks you routinely handle. Realize that 80% of your results come from 20% of your talents and activities. Delegate the 80% of your activities that only produce 20% of your results. Stop doing the wrong kind of work. CEOs should think, lead and delegate -- not handle trivial matters. Your job as CEO is to design/re-design and grow the business; your managers' job is to improve the business; and your employees' job is to operate the business. Here are a few more suggestions:

    - No longer major in minor things! Don't let yourself get distracted by irrelevant, insignificant stuff.
    - Don't let the urgent control your life. Put your cell phone/pager away more often. Don't be a prisoner to email.
    - Instead of creating a to-do list, start creating a **not-to-do** list for you and let go of small things. Eliminate or delegate the 80% of your activities that produce so little impact for your business. Share this not-to-do list with your team. Put them on notice that you are getting out of the daily detail (usually their areas of responsibility) and starting to see and influence the big picture.
    - Quit trying to manage details and start managing your people. Guide their focus and priorities, but let them do the work.

5. Schedule time to think and plan. You must think deeply about important, strategic matters. Make time to get away from the day-to-day distractions and focus on deep thinking, planning, and decision-making. Isolate yourself to concentrate on big-picture issues. Spend time alone digesting all the information you are bombarded with and develop the big ideas to take your business to the next level of performance. Once a month, schedule a day away from

the office to think and plan. With no distractions whatsoever, put on your CEO hat and spend time reviewing and improving your chief asset – your business.

6. On a daily basis, reserve the vast bulk of the day to tackle only your top 3 priorities. Selfishly guard your time and focus. Don't allow your employees to disrupt your CEO-oriented priorities and actions with countless got-a-minute interruptions. Allowing such conduct creates an environment whereby your time is not valued and respected. It also creates unproductive days, a reactive business mindset and employees that are overly dependent upon you for everything. Stop these got-a-minute interruptions.

7. Think about CEO role models at large companies you admire. Those proven CEOs with solid integrity and ethics. For example, think of the former CEO at GE, Jack Welch. Read his books and understand his philosophies, mindset, and strategies. Then periodically stop yourself and ask, "What would a Jack Welch do in this case?"

8. Whatever your technical expertise, consider hiring someone else to handle such technical and tactical work so that you can escape the stranglehold. For example, if your background is selling or accounting, hire a competent sales manager or accounting manager to manage such day-to-day details. If you already have such employees on your payroll, then for goodness sakes let them do their jobs. Get out of their zone of responsibility.

9. And finally, adopt a mindset of optimization (see the next section).

Adopt the Mindset of Optimization

As a CEO, you need to elevate your mindset and obsess about getting more from your current resources and efforts. You must ask yourself and others better questions. You must start to ask yourself, "How can our business get greater results from every action we take, every expenditure we make, every effort we expend, every relationship we have?" Avoid status quo like a deadly virus. You must embrace fully the philosophies that, "good enough never is" and "we can always do better."

Optimization (also known as leverage) is a mindset of maximizing your results while simultaneously minimizing the amount of time, effort, risk, money, and energy you expend. It's all about getting greater productivity, performance, profitability and payback from your ideas, assets, knowledge, systems, processes, practices, people and opportunities. Overlook nothing; leverage opportunities are everywhere.

Optimization is all about using your mind and limited business resources in new and better ways. It's about using your creative intelligence as an incredible force to increase your sales, customer satisfaction, profits, quality, etc. Optimization is about freeing yourself and your organization from limiting beliefs, the "we've always done it this way" attitudes, and established industry practices. Optimization is searching for opportunities inside and outside your company where the application of focus or force will yield substantially multiplied results. For example, if you start using telephone calls to follow-up your direct mail campaigns, you may multiply your sales results by staggering amounts.

Just as a tire jack can lift the tremendous weight of a car for a tire change, so too can the strategy of optimization help you significantly lift your company's revenues, improve operations, and lighten your daily load. A lever, fulcrum and slight force can lift significant weight if you know how to use these tools. Learn about leverage so you can begin to elevate and optimize your business results.

To master the art of optimization, you need to adopt an opportunity mindset. To leave the status quo behind, you need to ask continually the following types of questions:

- What is the best and highest use of our time, talent, and treasures?
- What resources are we underutilizing?
- How can we maximize our returns/output and minimize our input?
- How can we work smarter, not harder?
- Which strategies will give us super-sized results?
- What processes or departments within our business are under-performing?
- What past or current relationships could we more fully leverage (i.e. customers, employees, vendors, suppliers, advisers, etc.)?
- What other industries could provide us with some innovative best practices?
- Where are the hidden opportunities within our business, our employees, our suppliers/vendors, our business partners, our customer base, our competitors, and our business processes?
- How can we get a greater return/payoff using the least amount of money, time, risk, etc?
- How can we be more effective, more productive?
- How can we get better every day in every way?
- What suggestions from our customers should we pursue first?

Expand your mind and your leadership potential and your business and opportunities expand exponentially. The more you grow as a leader, the more your business grows as a market leader. The quality of your business and your personal life will depend on the quality of your leadership. Think CEO, not employee. Think optimization, not status quo. Much more on leadership will be discussed in the fifth chapter, Maximizing Your Leadership.

Now that you understand how to think and behave like a CEO, it is time to systematize your business for smoother operations. For your company to function at its best and not rely on you for every decision and action, you must put robust business systems in place. The systems give you the freedom to function as a CEO.

Suggested Action Items:

- Great transformations begin in and with the mind. Pledge to yourself that you will be open to change. Acknowledge that all lasting and effective change begins on the inside. Believe in the BE-DO-HAVE goal-achievement formula.
- What percentage of a typical day do you spend working **in** the business versus **on** the business? Stated another way, determine what percentage of the typical day you function as an employee instead of a strategic business owner.
- Admit to yourself and your coach that you can no longer tolerate being an employee; you must function as a CEO. Using the term CEO will force you to see your company as an entity above and beyond yourself, as a separate and valuable asset that needs to be professionally handled and optimized. Concentrate working **on** the business, not **in** the business. Consider putting CEO on your business cards, letterhead, nameplate, etc.
- Your job as CEO is to design (or re-design) and grow the business; your managers' job is to improve the business; and your employees' job is to operate the business. Again, your goal is to design and build a business that serves you and works without you -- a business that is systems-dependent and not owner-dependent. You want a business that runs

nearly on autopilot and spits out cash. Ensure that your to-do list and your not-to-do list reflect this new reality.

- Get out of your technical comfort zone and get into your CEO zone. Admit to yourself and your coach what your comfort zone challenge will be (i.e. selling, accounting, marketing, product development, etc.). Pledge to move away from this technical bias.

- How do you stop thinking like an employee? Change your metaphors about being a business owner. For example, instead of seeing yourself as a key player, see yourself as the head coach. Other metaphors could be director, leader, conductor, etc.

- To help with this mindset transformation to CEO, start viewing your company as a valuable asset separate and apart from you that requires professional management and care to grow it. Spend time and energy helping to build, improve and optimize this asset -- the business.

- To help with this mental transformation, consider that as CEO, you get paid $200 an hour to professionally manage this separate entity and asset – your business. Ask yourself before you touch any task, "Would a CEO do this?" Or ask, "Is this task worth me doing it at a cost of $200 an hour?" Or ask, "Is this an important task or merely an urgent yet unimportant task?"

- No longer major in minor things! Stop doing the wrong kind of work. Don't let yourself get distracted by irrelevant, insignificant stuff. Eliminate or delegate 80% of your activities that produce only 20% of your results. Create a not-to-do list (low value, low priority, urgent tasks) for yourself as CEO and share it with your team. Put them on notice about which activities you will no longer conduct. Train others to tackle such tasks. Focus on the 20% of your talents and activities that produce the bulk of your results!

- Focus on your top 3 CEO priorities every day. Don't tolerate endless "got-a-minute" interruptions. Don't be unapproachable. Rather, educate your employees how to schedule time with you for more proactive and productive meetings.

- Schedule a day a month away from the office, with no distractions whatsoever. Put on your CEO hat and spend time reviewing and improving your chief asset – your business.
- Start asking yourself, "What would the CEO at GE, IBM, McDonalds, etc. do in this situation?"
- Hire others to replace you in the technical trenches of your business.
- Adopt a mindset of optimization.
- Believe your company can get better every day in every way. Maximize your results while minimizing your company's output of time, effort, risk and money. Pledge to get greater results from every action you take, every expenditure you make and every relationship you have.
- Repeatedly ask the optimization-type questions that appear on page 32. Photocopy such questions and keep them on your desk, in your truck, at home, etc.
- Ask all your internal and external stakeholders, "How can we improve _____ and get greater results?"

SHAPING YOUR BUSINESS NOW TO BE SOLD LATER

Points to Ponder

- *Organizations are perfectly designed for the results they achieve. Want new results, get a new design.*
  Paul Gustavson
- *First comes thought; then organization of that thought into ideas and plans; then transformation of those plans into reality. The beginning as you will observe, is in your imagination.*
  Napoleon Hill
- *Genius is the ability to reduce the complicated to the simple.*
  C.W. Ceram
- *A good system shortens the road to the goal.*
  Orison Swett Marden
- *Success or failure is often determined on the drawing board.*
  Robert J. McKain

Be a Sculptor to Strike it Rich

Now that we thoroughly discussed the importance of thinking and acting like a CEO, it is time for you to be a sculptor. Time to mold your business to run more efficiently, effectively and consistently. Don't let your business evolve haphazardly and reactively. Proactively shape it or re-shape it to make for smoother operations, consistent customer satisfaction and profitable results. You must turn chaos, confusion, and anarchy into order and discipline. Time to standardize and document your business.

Challenge your old beliefs about how your business should work. It is never too early to shape or too late to re-shape your business. It doesn't matter if your business is 20 years old, 2 years old, 2 months old or on the drawing board, start shaping the company to run without your being woven into the very fabric of the business. Design it to run without your supplying all the effort and energy. You cannot control everything, you cannot control everyone. Let go! Start behaving like a strategic business owner.

You do not want to create merely a job for yourself. The ultimate goal of creating a business is to sell it one day, at the highest premium possible, to your employees, family members, or an outside buyer. You deserve an acceptable return on your investment of time, talent, and treasure.

No matter what size, age or industry, every business should be prepared to be sold. Yours is no different. This "start with the end in mind" strategy should help you focus on building an effective business model that doesn't have you at the center of its universe, relying on your presence, personality and perspiration for its success. Again, you should not be the business and the business should not be you. This work-in-reverse approach not only maximizes your selling price, but also minimizes your hassles and headaches while you own and run the business.

As stated earlier, your goal is to design or re-design your business to work without you. Your business model should be sculpted in such a way that it can be easily replicated dozens of times in cities around the country or world, requiring only your vision, not your physical presence and exertion. Whether you ever expand or not, such an ambition should help you focus on building a systems-dependent (not owner-dependent or people-dependent) business that generates repeatable performance and consistent results. You must help others get results. Without other people, you don't run a business -- you work a job.

What is an effective business system? It is simply an integrated web of separate processes, procedures and policies. A business system allows you to get consistent results through other people – tremendous leverage and freedom! The business system is your documented instruction manual for "this is what and how we do it" at our company. Some typical operating processes are as follows:

- Selling
- Marketing
- Manufacturing
- Inventory management
- Order processing/customer fulfillment
- Customer service
- Billing and accounts receivable
- Procurement/accounts payable
- Facilities management
- Accounting/finance
- Human resources (i.e. hiring, firing, reviewing, promoting, paying, etc.)
- Information systems
- Store opening and closing procedures

Your business with such processes fully identified and explained will allow your employees to deliver amazing consistency. Employee discretion is minimized. Such a system will also free you from having to touch every transaction, make every decision, answer every question and solve every problem. You can manage by exception! Such a carefully crafted enterprise will also give you breathing space to think and act like a strategic business owner as well as the time to do personal activities that matter most to you.

Without such a business system in place, no one will want to pay a premium for your broken business. They would not want to buy a dysfunctional business that is solely dependent upon you for its day-to-day operations and survival. If it were obvious that you are a prisoner to your business, why would anyone want to buy into such a life sentence? They would not or would pay very little for such a systems-deficient business. Please grasp this; no one wants to buy a job, a series of headaches, or an owner-centered and owner-dependent business.

To maximize your company's eventual selling price, realize that buyers want to acquire a smoothly running, money-generating machine. Buyers want to purchase a business system that runs on near autopilot, foolproof status. They want to buy a fully documented, organized business system that gets predictable results. They want an asset that has proven processes, predictable revenue streams, and strong growth potential. They want to buy a well-designed, hassle-free, cash flowing asset, not a pain in the ass.

The more of a turnkey, self-managing, self-improving system you develop, the greater the value to a potential buyer. If your business runs well without your being there every day, it will be worth gold to others. And until the day you sell, don't you want to own and manage the same type of well-designed, well-orchestrated business?

The System is the Solution

During the early phase of business development or re-engineering, your brainpower and sweat equity should go into the design and creation of your business model and business systems – not into micro-managing. Spend time developing systems and performance standards early on so that you can lead later on. Design an entire business template. Define and organize the work to be done rather than micro-managing the employees. The more you systematize your business, the less everyone will rely on you for day-to-day questions and assistance. You will minimize those nagging "got-a-minute" interruptions from your employees. Also, the system you develop takes your place so that you can step out of the trenches and function as CEO. Replace yourself with the system!

Your mission is to plan and design the system and then let your employees work the system. Develop the recipe and then let the employees do the cooking! Get out of the hot kitchen. Your employees should understand their roles and function within and according to the system. Once defined and documented, processes, policies, and practices should be carefully followed.

With help from employees and your business advisers, identify and document all the processes, procedures and policies necessary to achieve more effective and streamlined operations. You want to get frank feedback at this stage to ensure that you have an effective business model laid out first before you start documenting your business system. Start with customers' perceived needs and work backwards re-designing your business so that it consistently and predictably fulfills the promises made to a customer during the selling process. Be sure all your back-office processes (accounting, finance, HR, technology, administration, etc.) are in alignment to effectively support the operations of the company. Design or repair any processes that are missing or faulty.

Routine work should be fully systematized and only exceptions should be dealt with on an impromptu or improvised basis. A system should eliminate arbitrary work and discretion. Your employees should have the discipline to follow the system and also have the freedom and authority to handle the exceptions that do not fit neatly into the system. Because most potential problems and crises have been properly anticipated and converted into routine processes, "fire drills" should be greatly reduced.

Once your system is fully documented and your employees are running the system, you need to let go, trust the system, trust your team, and step away from the day-to-day workflow. With this approach, twelve-hour days no longer need to be the norm. Once you allow the integrated system to run, the system itself and your employees will do the necessary work to fulfill promises made to your customers. You will not have to work as hard or as long. With effective systems, ordinary employees (properly trained) can achieve consistently extraordinary results.

The system is your solution to more freedom, fulfillment, and profits. Again, plan and develop the system and let others operate the system.

How to Systematize Your Business

Again, your overriding objective is to identify and document your company's key processes and practices in order to develop an operation manual/recipe for your employees to follow. In the end, you want to present current and future employees with a detailed user's manual for their jobs, with roles and expectations clearly spelled out.

Follow these six steps to shape your business system and develop your freedom-generating operations manual:

1. Don't rush or panic. Give yourself 4-6 months to finish your operations manual that captures (in print or electronically) every facet of your business and clearly explains "this is what and how we do it here." Oversee the process; don't do the work yourself.
2. Ensure that all processes, practices and policies are in place and functioning properly (i.e. selling, marketing, order processing/customer fulfillment, etc.). If necessary, use business advisers to ensure that your current business model has proper processes and practices in place to allow for streamlined and consistent operations. Based on this objective assessment, repair any defective processes and add

ones that are missing. In other words, make sure to capture all the ingredients and steps before finalizing the recipe.

3. Once you have all the right processes in place, have your employees document like crazy. Have your current employees write down their roles, job descriptions, and daily, weekly, and monthly responsibilities. If you yourself wear multiple hats, define and document the best way to do your various roles. Then replace yourself with someone else.

4. Have departmental managers write down their department's role, responsibilities, and daily, weekly, and monthly tasks. Also, have them document all the key processes relevant to their department (i.e. selling, operations, etc.).

5. Assign a champion to work with other managers to document your organization's company-wide (multi-department) processes that have not yet been addressed. For example, customer service most likely needs to be tackled by several department managers as it spans multiple functional areas.

6. If necessary, hire an expert in organizational design or workflow enhancement and documentation to make the validation of your business system and creation of your operations manual a reality.

These six steps will not only document "this is what and how we do it here" but will also reveal under-utilized employees, problems in your workflow, and general areas to improve. Unless you know how something currently operates, you cannot begin to measure it or improve it. Without specific tasks clearly defined, it's nearly impossible to delegate. Furthermore, as your people work the system, coach them to think about continually improving the system. Such innovation ensures that the business gets better and better.

I'm sure you worry that such documentation will require a great deal of work, time or money. You are absolutely right! However, you can do it right once and have a smoothly running, easy-to-manage company or ignore this advice and forever suffer from the consequences – being overloaded, a prisoner to your business, perpetually putting out fires, answering the same-old questions and handling the same-old issues in a grueling, re-active, off-the-cuff manner. Without a system, you will be continually barraged by employees visiting or calling you with got-a-minute interruptions. You can either pay the price now and regain your sanity, or continue to pay the price over the life of your ownership.

Don't get caught trying to do this all on your own. As the leader, your role is to oversee the process and creation of the master guide. Do not do it yourself! Lead the process and get expert help if necessary.

The name of the system game is documentation and continual improvement. After the initial documentation blitz, you should spend one hour a week with your team conducting workshops on process improvement. Review the documented processes, practices and policies and look for ways to repair, improve and optimize. By continually improving your processes, your business gets better and your customers get better service and value.

And finally, an operations manual creates other benefits for your company as well:

- The company is not dependent on any one employee possessing knowledge about certain processes, policies or practices. No single employee can hold the company hostage by what she knows.
- If an employee is out sick or leaves, he will not take all the knowledge out the door with him.
- As you grow and add more people, your operations manual will serve as an efficient and effective training and development tool.

- Employees will not need to come to you with unending questions, problems, and issues. You do not need to be the all-knowing, all-seeing oracle. They have the answer book and can seek out solutions on their own.
- Your business will not be owner-dependent, people-dependent or expert-dependent (most expensive, most experienced talent) to achieve consistent results.
- Imagine the day when a potential buyer holds this operations manual in their hands and can see first-hand an overview of every key process in your company and a detailed description of "this is how we do it here". They will see a unique, proprietary business model that really works. You will see a big fat juicy check with your name on it!
- With proper business documentation in place, you will not need to hire the most experienced, most expensive managers or key employees. Since the operations of the business are captured, you can focus on hiring people that will be hard working, loyal, and follow the game plan you have in place.

The Franchise Model for Validation

Need more convincing to start with the end in mind? Need more motivation to properly shape your business now to be successfully sold down the road? Let's look at the probability of success for most businesses.

Think about this. Why do such a large percentage (some say as much as 90%) of franchise businesses survive? It's because they come with a turnkey, fully documented operations manual and proven system that works regardless of the location and people involved. Successful franchise models are finely tuned systems-dependent businesses. They are the epitome of a strategic business.

They have perfected the way to do every key process (hiring people, selling, marketing, advertising, inventory management, facilities design, customer service, real estate selection and development, product fulfillment, etc.) and they have put it down on paper. A franchise is an entire business-system-in-a-box. You get a success recipe from the very start – a blueprint of a proven business model. That's why most franchise businesses succeed! Why not borrow the success strategies of this industry?

A franchise provides a buyer (franchisee) with an entire integrated operating system of doing business -- a proprietary and documented model of "how everything works here". It's entrepreneurship with a built-in safety net. The business owner gets an invaluable advantage -- she gets an owner's manual, an operations manual and an employee manual from day one. Everyone, including the owner, knows her role, responsibilities and performance expectations – they are clear and written down! That's why most franchise businesses thrive.

Without a proven business model or formula, most businesses fail. According to the Department of Commerce, more than 80% of U.S. businesses fail in the first five years. Another 80% of those survivors fail or decide to shut down in years 6-10. Why do 96 out of 100 businesses fail to see their 11th anniversary? It's simple; they have a technician's mindset and inadequate business systems, leadership, planning and marketing. In a nutshell, they are not strategic business owners.

By default, without a business system, companies and employees simply wing it – very little is planned and organized. There is minimal orchestration. Actions are arbitrary and random. The business depends on people instead of systems. There is no "this is how we do it" manual. Everyone is busy being busy. Everyone is caught in a purely reactive and fatiguing 911 emergency-response cycle. Owners and employees alike drain their precious energy improvising most tasks and get burned out recreating the wheel every day.

With everyone scrambling and "doing their own thing", no one is leading and directing -- the business just drifts. Most owners experience persistent exhaustion and blues and eventually close the doors. I'm convinced that most businesses don't fail because of bad concepts. Based on my experiences, most owners simply get run down and then give up. They decide the price to pay is too high.

Want to ensure your company's success and your sanity? If so, start designing or re-designing your business to be systems-oriented and self-managing. Why not borrow and adapt the success strategies of the franchise model? You do not want a business that is owner-dependent or people-dependent to achieve consistent results. You want a systems-dependent business that runs on autopilot. Life will be much easier while you are the owner and life will be much richer when you sell your business.

With a CEO mindset and an integrated business system in place, you will now have time and energy to focus on leadership, business planning, marketing, and people management.

Suggested Action Items:

- Understand and adopt the metaphor that you are a business sculptor or architect. Your job as CEO is to design and shape your business to be systems-dependent, not owner-dependent, not people-dependent, and not expert-dependent. You are to sculpt a business system that works without you at the center of its very heart and soul. You must design for and build in your freedom.

- Agree that franchises are successful in large part because they are a complete business-system-in-a-box. Pledge to borrow the success strategies of this industry.
- Fully embrace the following statements as a personal pledge: The ultimate goal of creating a business is to sell it one day to your employees, family members, or an outside buyer. To maximize your selling price, remember that no one wants to buy a job. They want to buy a smoothly running, effective, money-generating machine. They want to buy a successful, well-documented, organized business system that gets consistent results. Commit to yourself and your coach that you will shape your business now to be sold later!
- Have you designed your business to operate consistently and smoothly without your being at the heart of every decision and transaction? If not, admit the need to re-shape your business to be more systems-dependent and less owner-dependent. Share this revelation with your coach.
- Ask your coach to hold you accountable for starting the re-shaping, systematization and documentation process.
- Follow the six-step process on pages 42 and 43 to shape your business system and create your operations manual.
- If necessary, hire experts to assist with optimizing, documenting and/or continually improving your business processes.
- The name of the system game is documentation and continual improvement. After the initial documentation blitz, you should spend one hour a week with your team conducting workshops on process improvement. Review the documented processes, practices and policies and look for ways to repair, improve and optimize.
- Once you have created your operations manual, trust the business system you put in place and let go. This "business blueprint" should liberate you by being used to:
  - Train and develop new hires

- Greatly minimize employee interruptions and questions -- re-direct them to the operations manual
- Cover the gaps when employees are out sick or leave the company
- Prevent employees from re-creating the wheel – most recurring issues, problems, and crises should have been appropriately anticipated and handled within the routine processes you created in this operations manual

.

MAXIMIZING YOUR LEADERSHIP

Points to Ponder

- *Visualize this thing that you want. See it, feel it, believe in it. Make your mental blueprint and begin to build.*

  Robert Collier

- *The task of a leader is to get his people from where they are to where they have not been.*

  Henry Kissinger

- *Cherish your visions and your dreams as they are the children of your soul; the blueprints of your ultimate achievements.*

  Napoleon Hill

- *A leader is a dealer in hope.*

  Napoleon I

- *No one can whistle a symphony. It takes an orchestra to play it.*

  H. E. Luccock

After you begin to think and act like a CEO as well as systematize and document your business, you can step out of the daily detail and go to work **on** the remaining strategic areas: leadership, business planning, marketing, people management, and learning to let go.

This chapter will offer a crash course on leadership development. Once you have your operations manual/business recipe in writing, you will gain sufficient freedom to concentrate on growing your leadership abilities. In turn, as you expand your leadership mindset and skillsets, your business will expand proportionally. By leading more and working less, your joy will multiply and your blues will decrease.

Fight the urge to be all things to your company. If you are wearing multiple hats, you are being diverted from your chief responsibility, leadership. Increasing your leadership effectiveness will have a greater positive impact on your business than any other single factor. It will lift the shackles off the organization and free up your employees' potential. Since working harder is probably not even an option for you, why don't you try leading more? Again, if you don't lead, no one will.

Leadership is Everything to Your Business

If you learn nothing else from this book, fully understand and appreciate that leadership is everything to the success of an organization, whether a business, a house of worship, a political party, a school, a sports team, a family, a non-profit cause, or a volunteer organization. Leadership is the heart and soul of an organization. As the leadership goes, so goes the organization. Your business is no different. More important to your company's success than intelligence quotient (IQ) will be your LQ – Leadership Quotient!

Want to judge the upside potential of any organization, including yours? Look no further than the leader. Leadership, more than anything else, will determine the success or failure of a group or enterprise. The reason is simple. Every organization has a leadership ceiling.

An organization can rise only to the level of the owner's leadership capacity. The lower the leadership ceiling, the less room for everyone inside the organization to stretch and grow. Individuals cannot maximize their potential if a leader is holding them down and stunting their growth. If your people are suppressed, so is the potential of the business. Therefore, to grow your company, you must grow as a leader and grow the potential of your employees.

You are only as good as your people and systems. Without question, the better the leader, the better the business.

Like most of the topics in this book, leadership is a between-the-ears kind of issue. Like any skill, it can be learned and improved. Become a student of leadership. To be the best leader you can be, you must study the best. If possible, observe and emulate effective leaders. If role models are scarce, read about great leaders (political, religious, educational, scientific, cause-oriented, etc.), great coaches and great business executives. Study their philosophies, mindsets, habits and strategies. Borrow from their brilliance. Adopt and adapt those lessons that seem appropriate to your situation.

Like any worthwhile skill, leadership is also worth doing less than perfect in the beginning. Allow yourself a learning curve and the chance to develop and make mistakes. To be a leader, you must think like a leader and start acting like a leader.

Since thousands of books already focus exclusively on leadership, this chapter will serve to provide a mere overview of business leadership fundamentals. If necessary, seek additional leadership development assistance from books, tapes, seminars, and educational and business organizations.

Are you committed to elevating and expanding your leadership quotient? Are you up to the challenge? If so, look at business ownership as a wonderful journey of self-discovery and self-improvement. It is your real-world classroom for accelerated leadership development. And as a more effective and caring leader, you will positively impact your bottom-line results and the lives of countless individuals inside and outside your organization.

Remember, what you become as a business owner and leader is much more important and meaningful than what you achieve or possess. Through your leadership, you will make a significant difference to others. Make becoming a better leader one of your personal quests and a higher purpose for owning your business.

Leadership 101

What does a leader look like, sound like and do? There is no one correct mold. Great leaders come in all shapes, sizes, voices and styles. However, great leaders share a common outcome – they oversee getting important things done!

While leadership is hard to define, you know it when you see it, feel it, and hear it. An effective leader creates clarity about where the business is headed and how each team member can contribute to the cause. Such clarity helps reduce confusion and wasted actions and energy. Clarity also helps your employees to make better decisions within established boundaries. As a result, you can breathe more and supervise less.

Additionally, a leader motivates individuals to work together optimally as a team for a common cause or vision. A real leader pulls others along rather than push others around. Leadership is about communicating, not shouting out commands. You cannot coerce people to follow you for long. Command-and-control leaders seldom earn the hearts, minds and will of others.

Real leadership is all about influence, the ability to make others want to follow you and your cause. Proof of leadership is found in the loyalty and commitment level of your followers. When you turn around, are your employees eagerly and energetically following you and your vision? If not, commit to improving as a leader.

In addition to creating clarity of purpose and direction for the organization, a leader also creates the right conditions and climate for her team to succeed. It's simple; you cannot succeed on your own. You need energized and committed followers as much as they need an effective leader. It's a partnership in pursuit of a common cause. You are nothing without engaged followers. It's a symbiotic relationship – a leader needs his followers to get important things done.

To help you develop a solid foundation of knowledge, here is a list of some fundamental leadership practices:

A Leader Creates Clarity of Purpose & Direction by:

- Knowing where the company is going and why
- Developing and articulating a compelling vision for the business
- Selling the benefits of this vision to employees with facts, emotions, stories, symbols, etc.
- Establishing direction, strategies, and objectives for the company
- Developing a simple business plan
- Defining roles for and responsibilities of your employees
- Establishing clear expectations for individuals
- Developing processes to hold employees accountable for getting results
- Encouraging individuals to work as a team; elevating the needs of the team over the needs of the individual
- Focusing employees on key priorities and results (organizational focus)
- Setting standards, monitoring performance and giving feedback
- Reminding everyone that the business exists to serve and satisfy customers as well as to earn a healthy profit
- Influencing the thoughts, feelings and behavior of employees

A Leader Creates the Right Conditions (climate, culture) for Success by:

- Being a true leader (CEO), not another employee – taking the time to think, plan, see the big picture, and solve problems
- Building and maintaining a strong, healthy team
- Marshalling resources to support the strategy of the business
- Allowing others to do their jobs, not micro-managing them
- Allowing employees to share ideas and in the decision-making process – avoiding command-and-control leadership
- Getting others to believe in themselves and the mission of the company
- Serving and caring for others – being a giver, not a taker
- Getting the right people on board and the wrong people off
- Establishing a goal-oriented environment
- Maintaining open and honest communication; being open to positive and negative feedback
- Helping the company to face reality – the good, the bad and the ugly
- Accepting 100% responsibility for the results of the business
- Being bold and decisive even in the face of limited information
- Driving out fear of mistakes; encouraging experimentation and innovation
- Teaching and motivating others to reach their potential
- Monitoring financial performance and taking decisive action, when necessary
- Maintaining a positive culture through interviewing, hiring, reviewing and rewarding the right type of employees
- Ensuring the company is a fun place to work
- Being a competent, caring and connected leader of good character
- Creating a sense of urgency

A company without a leader is like a sports team without a head coach and without a game plan. Both scenarios will result in players (employees) doing their own selfish thing, running around without a purpose, with no sense of accountability, making repeated mistakes, posting lackluster performance, and most likely losing the game.

Your business doesn't need more defensive linemen; it needs an in-charge head coach. Let your employees do the daily "blocking and tackling". Create the game plan and let your employees play the game. Watch and coach from the sidelines, do not get in the trenches – you will lose vision of the whole field. Focus on creating clarity and conditions for success for your team.

You Are 100% Responsible

Look around your business. Whatever you like and dislike about your business and personal life is because of you. Whatever your business has become or failed to become is because of you. As the business owner, whether you like it or not, you are the de facto leader. Your business is what it is, where it is, and how it is because of you. Period. You are the leader. You are 100% responsible. You are the CEO, whether you are a company of one, 100, or 1,000. You are responsible for the good, the bad, and the ugly results and conditions of your business.

As such, do not blame your challenges, frustrations or problems on who is in the White House, the economy, interest rates, changing technology, globalization, industry trends, your employees, or your competition. Do not allow yourself to make excuses or blame others. Such a weakness will rob you of proper self-analysis and improvement. You will point to others for your problems and solutions instead of yourself and your team.

As leader, you are the solution to most everything that ails your company. Again, you are responsible for setting the direction and goals of the company and holding your team accountable for executing the game plan. You are responsible for shaping, systematizing and leading a business that is profitable and efficient. Unless you hire a professional business manager or President with full authority to run the business, leadership cannot be delegated. There is no such thing as effective leadership by committee or consensus. Every business needs and craves one strong leader with one clear vision. Get up and get going!

Creating the Vision

Jack Welch, former CEO of General Electric, has stated, "Good business leaders create a vision, articulate the vision, passionately own the vision, and relentlessly drive it to completion." Clear visions have helped shape and propel impressive companies. For example, Fred Smith, founder of Federal Express, had a vision that packages could be delivered around the United States by the next morning. Disney wanted to make families smile. Dominoes wanted you to have hot, delicious pizza delivered to your door in 30 minutes or less or it was free. Coke wanted to have its refreshing beverages within the reach of every person in the world. Microsoft wanted to create beneficial software that would compel people to have a computer on every desk at work, home and school.

Jonathan Swift said, "Vision is the art of seeing things invisible." Don't sell vision creation short. You must learn to understand, value, and appreciate the essential role of an exciting vision for a healthy and growing business. Start thinking and planning more. Escape the tyranny of the urgent and focus on one of the most important tasks you can do – create an exciting future destiny and direction for your business. Effective visions also help lead the leaders – keeping them motivated and challenged.

Let me state a warning. Fully realize that your employees must buy into you as a leader before they buy into your vision. They must believe and trust in you to believe and trust in your vision. You may need to do some repair work to establish yourself as a caring and competent leader before you start creating and selling your vision. You will need to connect with their hearts before connecting with their heads.

To create a new vision or sharpen and update an existing one, allow yourself a month. See yourself as the Chief Listening Officer during this early phase. You cannot build a vision or business on your own. For buy-in later, seek the input of others now. Include your employees, customers, suppliers, distributors and business advisers in the process. Spend a week or two gathering input from these stakeholders about your company's direction, strengths, weaknesses, threats and opportunities. If they do not participate in this creation phase, they will not want to participate in the vision implementation phase. Also, study your industry trends and your current and emerging competitors. On all fronts, do your homework.

After listening to and studying others, be certain to listen to your inner voice and gut. While other's input is critical, know that the buck stops with you. You are ultimately responsible for the vision of your business. Your vision ultimately becomes your company's direction, objectives, priorities, strategies, and tactics. It is that magical and that important.

Therefore, get away from the daily interruptions and go into your *CEO Cave*. This could be your home office, at a coffee shop, at a park, library or beach. Spend two to three days forming or crystallizing a picture of what you want the business to look like in one year, three years, and five years. See things the way they can be. Dream the big dream; unleash your spirit. See the business in your heart that you truly want to create. A bold, daring, super-sized vision, even if only partially achieved, yields greater rewards than a small, wimpy vision fully achieved.

Remember, there are no rules while you create a desired future state. However, don't deal in pure fantasy. There is a difference between a vision and a delusion. Stay somewhat grounded. You must see things the way they are now in order to visualize the way they can be. You must build from a foundation of realism, acknowledging your company's current strengths, weaknesses, opportunities and threats. However, once you gather the facts, let go and let her rip.

Grab hold of the future, bring it into the present, and then go about creating it. Give yourself and your employees something to be proud of. Find a voice to express the common dreams, emotions, potential and needs of your team. Let your vision inspire, motivate, and galvanize your team. Small visions do not stir the soul. Give people a reason to follow, something to shoot for. Make the vision intoxicating -- something that captures their imagination. Show them the finish line in bright, Technicolor detail. Sell more to their hearts than to their heads. People change when their feelings change, not when merely their thoughts change. Powerful visions unite groups and take them to new heights and places.

Keep in mind, employees want purpose and passion to lift them and propel them. Find a larger purpose for your company than merely making money. Don't settle for being a random collection of people and assets trying to make a buck. A purely financial focus will not sustain the troops over the long term. Make coming to work a meaningful and fulfilling event for your employees. People want to work in a challenging and rewarding environment. They want to learn, grow and reach their potential – the full expression of their talent. People are drawn to great leaders, great visions and great causes.

Having trouble thinking big? Ask yourself bigger questions!

- Why does our enterprise exist?
- If our business were shut down, what would be missing in this world?
- What is our crusade? What could be our crusade?
- How do we engage the hearts, minds and souls of our employees?
- How can we make our company great, meaningful and different?
- How can we change our industry, community, and even the world?
- How can we measurably improve the lives of customers?
- How can we make our employees and their families' lives better and more fulfilling?
- What higher calling or spiritual dimension can we embrace?

After listening to others for two weeks and thinking deeply yourself for two weeks, a vision for your company should be coming into focus. Bottom line, this vision should help your employees and yourself re-acquire the fire and passion for your company's direction and purpose.

Selling the Vision

Once you establish a vivid image of your desired future business, you then must share continually and passionately this dream with your team. After all, a vision without execution is a hallucination. Now, see yourself as the Chief Enthusiasm Officer or Chief Storytelling Officer as you must effectively sell the direction of your company.

Don't be afraid to sell emotionally. Again, you must win hearts, minds and wills. People change when their feelings change, not when their thoughts change. Make them feel differently. Help them feel what you feel – your passion, hope and optimism. Help them want what you want. You must translate the vision into real terms and achievable steps. You must transfer a picture of your vision into the hearts, minds and souls of your employees.

Time to start selling the vision, telling the story. From hereon out, it's not only what you say, it's how you say it that matters. Be dramatic and be memorable with your talks on the vision. Use a combination of facts, emotions, stories, pictures and symbols to get your point across. Don't worry; you cannot over-communicate your vision. Your employees deserve and crave to know your heart's desires. Keep them informed, involved and inspired. Be a persuasive storyteller. Let employees know what you see in the future regarding your company's:

- Competitive position
- Sales and profit trends
- Market share penetration
- Number of employees
- Number of locations
- Geographic reach
- Type of customers/clients served
- Dominant niches
- Industry standing
- Product/service innovations
- Sales and marketing processes
- Structure, business systems, work flow
- Strategic alliances
- Office environment

Get everyone to see and move toward this ideal business model. Such clarity eliminates confusion and wasted time and energy. Once everyone knows the vision, they will have an internal blueprint to guide their daily behaviors and decisions. It is easier for your team to grasp and move toward a clearly communicated vision than a cold, impersonal, 40-page strategic plan. Facts do not flame faith. A compelling vision (business story) will stoke the fires of faith and passion.

You aren't a charismatic leader you say. You don't need to be! Pick a leadership style that works for you. You can be introverted and still be effective. However, you must have imagination to dream and see, taste, and feel the vision. You must be an effective communicator to share this compelling future. You must be a storyteller in order to sell your vision, sell the hope. You must have unswerving conviction and enthusiasm for the dream. Do not be afraid to use metaphors, stories or symbols to shorten the communication path. For example, if you see your company as nimble, fast and competitive, consider using a shark or cheetah to make your point easier to understand.

While communicating the vision to others, never underestimate the influence of your actions. Put bluntly, your actions speak louder than your words. How you spend your money, allocate your time and resources say more than any words. Are your actions in alignment with your vision? Your employees know this. In fact, they know where your heart is by following where your wallet is and where your time is spent. For example, if your vision includes having superior customer service yet you cut corners or do not pay for your employees to be properly trained in such matters, do you think they will embrace your vision? No. Put your money and your attention where your vision is.

In addition to sharing your vision, you must be adroit at developing systems and organizational structure that support this vision. In short, you must be a business architect. While the vision is the foundation of your business, you must be able to build the walls, roof, plumbing system, etc. Your marketing, selling, operations, and infrastructure must align with your vision. As stated earlier, after you define the business, your managers should help develop the system, and your employees should run the system.

And lastly, consider sharing your vision externally with your business advisers, investors, suppliers, and customers. Be proud of your vision and let everyone know you are a dynamic, focused, energized organization. The more they are aligned with your business, the more powerful your company.

It's All About Focus

It's been said that managers do things right and leaders do the right things. The former is about efficiency the latter is about effectiveness. It is easy to be busy but hard to work on the right things. Leaders must focus on doing the right things -- those things that matter most to the success of the company. In short, effective leaders must drive the focus of the organization. Leaders must channel the time, talent, energy, and resources of the organization on tackling key priorities and goals. Owners must ask constantly, "What's Important Now (WIN)?"

In today's fast-paced, technology connected world, it's easy for people to lose track of what is most important to the enterprise. They get so caught up in the day-to-day minutia and distractions (email, voicemail, cell phones, PDAs, etc.) that they must be re-directed, re-focused, re-oriented continually. Owners need to rein in their employees' focus. Do not let your employees waste energy, time, talent, and resources on trivial matters; keep them focused on the company's vision and its mission-critical priorities.

To help you manage the attention and concentration of your team, consider focusing them on six primary areas:
1. Satisfying your customers/clients
2. Getting results, not excuses
3. Improving continuously (innovation)

4. Maintaining profits
5. Keeping a long-term perspective
6. Having fun

1) Focus on satisfying your customers

Your company's primary focus should be squarely on exceeding the expectations of your customers/clients. Begin to establish a culture whereby your team falls in love with your customers and their needs/wants and not your own company's products or services. You are in business to attract, delight and retain customers in a profitable manner – period. The real value of your business is tied directly to the future, predictable cash flow from your highly satisfied and loyal customers. Without customers, you do not have a business.

Again, your focus should be on your customers and solving their needs and wants. It should not be about your company or your services and products. Teach your employees to value your customers, serve them well, and sniff out any customer problems or complaints. Keep your customers delighted and coming back for more! As leader, have the courage to create an environment in which the customer is your enterprise's primary focus.

As CEO, set the tone by visiting regularly the top 20% of your customers and keeping them satisfied. Find out what is on their minds. Aside from creating clarity of direction for your business, there is no better use of your time and talents.

2) Focus on getting results

Next, focus your team on achieving results for your company. Establish the climate whereby activity is not confused with accomplishment. Where thinking and planning are admired. Where actual results are valued more than busyness. Where effectiveness (doing the right things) is rewarded more than efficiency (doing things right). Insist on intelligent, meaningful action and detest procrastination (paralysis-by-analysis) and excuses. As a leader, one of the most important jobs you have is to establish a goal-oriented environment with a solid expectation of performance. Insist on results; do not tolerate excuses.

The chapter on business planning and implementation will cover how to set and achieve business goals.

3) Focus on continual improvement
After satisfying customers and insisting on results, the next focus area should be on continuous improvement. If your company is not improving, it is declining. If you aren't getting better, your competitors are getting stronger. Therefore, establish a climate where continuous improvement and innovation thrive. Do not let your employees fear failure or making mistakes. Just eliminate repeated mistakes. Failure is not fatal, but failing to change might be.

As CEO, you must drive out fear from your organization. If your company is not failing occasionally, either your goals are too low or your rate of innovation is too slow. Have your employees adopt the attitude that failure is not painful or shameful. Failure is merely valuable feedback on what not to do next time. Failure is fertilizer for future success. Failure is an incredible gift if properly viewed and used. If we are moving closer to our goals, we are winning. The quicker we fail and modify our approach, the quicker we get to our desired outcome.

Insist that your employees continually improve what they do and how they do it. Focus them on thinking about how to improve their roles, responsibilities, and contribution to the cause. Have them also improve your systems and processes. Remind them, "Good enough never is." Refer back to the theory of optimization for powerful questions to ask yourself and your team.

Encourage employees to try new things. Experiment, experiment, experiment! Insist that "we can always do better – let's find the way!" Take small steps to test ideas and learn more in the process. If something works better, keep it. If it doesn't, lose it. Know when to cut your losses. Admit mistakes and let go of failed ideas fast. Fail fast, fail cheap. Keep your ego in check.

Once a week, facilitate a one-hour business improvement workshop. Release the brainpower of your organization. For every good idea surfaced, assign a champion, due date, and key action steps to take. Good ideas not fully implemented are worthless. Reward employees for successfully implementing ideas that increase revenues, cut costs, improve operations or morale, or improve customer satisfaction.

Also, encourage healthy debate amongst your team. Allow everyone, in a constructive manner, to challenge ideas, policies and strategies. Even allow for productive and constructive conflict. When ideas are put to the test, they improve.

4) Focus on profits
Next, focus on growing your revenues and most importantly, your profits. Focus on both top line and bottom line growth. Focusing only on revenue growth is ego-driven and not too smart. Cash flow and profits are your lifeblood. Keep your gross margins strong.

Also, while cost containment is important to the health of your company, do not over-emphasize slashing costs. Stay on the offensive, not the defensive. Revenue growth is nearly endless, cost cutting is limited – you can only cut so much before you do real damage. Some costs are really strategic investments in the future of your business (new equipment, advertising, training & development, etc.) .

Give yourself a blessing. Hire the best CPA you can afford and one that not only understands numbers well, but the issues we are discussing in this book. An entrepreneurial-oriented CPA that understands the needs of a growing business and owner is invaluable – worth the premium!

5) Focus on the long-term
After profits, focus everyone on the fact that you are in business for the long haul. Do not be short-term oriented. Business is a marathon, not a sprint. Do what is right, always. Maintain the highest integrity and ethics. Your reputation is everything. Business is about sustaining lifelong relationships with customers, employees, investors, suppliers, advisers, etc. Repeat business is absolutely critical to the very life force of your company. Do not take shortcuts.

To help with this concept, consider the Lifetime Value of your customers. On average, how much profit does a typical customer provide you over the average service life (# of years) of such a customer? For example, if a typical company buys from you several times a year, yielding you a total annual profit of $1,000, and you generally retain such a customer for 5 years, the Lifetime Value for a typical customer is $5,000. Stated another way, every time you attract a new customer and serve them well, odds are that customer will be worth $5,000 to your business over time.

Once you know this number, you and your employees should think twice about upsetting a customer or losing a customer. This Lifetime Value also validates that you should spend money (acquisition cost) to attract new customers. As long as you break-even on acquiring a customer and know with certainty that there is considerable back-end or repeat business, it makes sense to spend money on marketing and selling. Invest a little to make a lot! That's leverage.

6) Focus on having fun
And lastly, focus on making business fun. Celebrate worthwhile progress toward your goals. Celebrate your company's successes often and reward your employees for superior performance. Come

up with excuses to praise your team and recognize success. Share the joy. Make coming to work a meaningful and fulfilling event. In fact, appoint a CFO (Chief Fun Officer). Empower this person to come up with clever ideas, based on employee feedback, which will put some excitement and fun into the work environment.

Never forget, often as important as a paycheck, good employees want to learn and grow, be challenged and rewarded, and fulfill their cravings to be social beings. Make your culture an enjoyable place to work.

Don't Micro-Manage

Real leadership is rare; micro-management is all too common. Stop trying to play every darn instrument yourself and start conducting the orchestra. If you don't conduct, who will?

Time for a fast refresher. As a strategic business owner, your primary aim should be to develop a self-managing and systems-oriented business that still runs consistently, predictably, smoothly, and profitably while you are not there. You should shape and own the business system and employ competent and caring employees to operate the system. You should document the work of your business so that you can effectively train others to execute the work. You must make yourself replaceable in the technical trenches of your business. To repeat, define and document the specific work to be done and then train and delegate. Don't suffocate the talents and growth of your employees.

Don't be a super-worker, be a supervisor! Stop the "I'll do it myself" and "No one does it as well as I do" attitudes. Learn to delegate. Engage your coach to help you with this critical skill.

If someone else can do something 80-90% as well as you, give it up! Do not spend a dollar's worth of time on a dime task. Know your areas of brilliance and delegate most everything else. Do those things that only you can do as CEO and delegate the rest. You need to free up time to do CEO activities that make the vision a reality. However, be sure to delegate, not abdicate or dump. Stay in touch with the person and their progress.

To help with delegation, you must have the work to be done well defined. You cannot delegate non-specifics. Next, you must adopt the attitude that your time is valuable and learn to discriminate between various activities. Before doing a task, ask, "Does this task lead directly to increased profits, significantly reduced costs, improved customer satisfaction, or to me building a better business?" If it doesn't, dismiss the task or delegate it. Or ask, "Is this task worth $200 per hour?" If not, find someone else internally or externally to do this task at a cheaper rate. You must realize that your CEO thoughts and actions (building systems, leading, planning, holding people accountable, coaching other leaders, etc.) are worth at least $200 per hour. If not, you will never learn to be effective at delegation.

By all means, get out of the way of your managers and workers. Don't meddle. Instead of doing their jobs, help them to clarify their roles, responsibilities, goals, and tasks and then simply hold them accountable for getting things done. Be sure to monitor your employees' performance, don't try to control them. Coach more and play less in the game.

Once they demonstrate competency and character, give your employees the authority to make things happen. Let them do their jobs. Let them tackle stuff on their own and come to you only when they need further guidance. Instead of micro-managing the process, manage by results. If you set up your systems correctly and train properly, you will be able to manage by numbers and on an exception-only basis.

I imagine and hope that you are paying your employees and managers good money to do their jobs. If so, get out of their way and let them perform. If you aren't paying adequate wages, beware! If you pay peanuts, then expect to attract monkeys.

Leadership is less about doing, more about thinking, planning, and overseeing what others do. You are to create jobs, not work a job.

Be Bold, Be Decisive

Followers want their leaders to be bold, focused and decisive. As such, make things happen! Do not get caught in the "ready, aim, aim, aim" loop. After sufficient thinking and analysis, have the guts to "fire", to make things happen. Here are some suggestions:

- Generally, inaction is more costly than action. Implementing a good idea today is usually a better strategy than waiting several months for a possible great idea.
- Most times, value movement over meditation, action over analysis.
- Even with limited information, continue to make decisions. Don't delay.
- Know where you are going and why.
- Listen to and trust your inner voice and instincts.
- Go for growth over status quo. Don't settle for the ordinary.
- Go for breakthroughs, not incremental changes.
- Write your own rules.
- Have a zeal for focusing on important goals and having a bias for action.
- Have a good plan but have great execution.

Keeper of Reality

As a leader, you are the keeper of reality and the seer of truth. One of your primary tasks is to help define reality, to remove the blinders, to expose blind spots, to reveal delusions.

Be neither a gushing optimist nor a panicked pessimist. Be a realist with undying faith in the potential and promise of your company. Know your company and your team's strengths, weaknesses, opportunities and threats. See your ever-changing situation for what it really is and not what it was or what you or others wish it to be. Do not allow delusions or blind spots to take your company down. Burn off the fog that is clouding an objective view. Armed with the facts and a strong dose of reality, you can always make necessary adjustments. Deal in fact, not fiction.

Share the Knowledge

Learn to share existing knowledge within your company and seek fresh ideas and strategies from without. Knowledge is power, but only if it is applied. The cumulative knowledge in your organization is immense. However, most businesses do not openly share knowledge, best practices, or mistakes.

If you do not create the right environment, people hoard knowledge and hide mistakes in order to possess power or avoid embarrassment. You must encourage an environment where all knowledge, good and bad, is to be shared. Very often, some of your most innovative ideas will come from people you least expect. Be committed to finding the best way, not in having your own way. Tap into everyone's brainpower.

As CEO, continually ask your employees:

- "If you were CEO for a day, what would you improve and why?"
- "Give me three ways for us to substantially grow our profits."
- "Give me three ways for us to dramatically improve our operations/customer fulfillment."
- "Give me three ways to dramatically improve our customer satisfaction rates."
- "Give me three ways for us to dramatically improve our office environment or team spirit."

At all costs, you must avoid mental constipation. Learning is leverage. As CEO, you need to meet with and learn from other entrepreneurial CEOs. Join CEO Roundtables via your Chamber of Commerce, the Young Entrepreneurs Organization (YEO), the Young Presidents Organization (YPO), or start your own CEO Mastermind Group. Find a mentor who has successfully mastered the company-building process and effective leadership. Again, use your coach to hold you accountable for learning, sharing and innovating.

Don't become myopic. Look beyond your industry for ideas. Consider how other industries are marketing, selling, operating, and working. Read trade magazines from different industries. Carry a notebook or mini-recorder to capture fresh ideas. As you expand your mind, so expands your options, possibilities, ideas, strategies, and your business.

Gather outside directors that can bring diversity, expertise, objectivity and experiences to your business. Add people who can raise issues, challenge you, and make suggestions. Consider dismissing those that can't.

And finally, hire top-notch advisors (CPA, banker, attorney, executive coach, specific consultants, etc.) and fire those that do not bring real value. Hire ones that specialize in working with fast-growing, entrepreneurial companies. Make sure they understand the concept of working "on" not "in" a business and understand the critical importance of leadership, business systems, planning, marketing, people management, and learning to let go. If so, they will more than pay for themselves.

Financial Stewardship

You must have a handle on the numbers. You should know constantly the financial health and trends of your organization. You must be able to look for ways to grow revenues and reduce costs. You must be able to understand an income statement, balance sheet, and cash flow statement and what they are telling you. Do not try to manage your business by gut instinct; the numbers never lie.

Learn about and monitor your company's vital signs. Have your Accounting Manager or CPA put together simple "dashboard metrics" to help you steer your business. Such metrics are simple, key measures that let you know the performance of your business at a glance. Depending on your company and industry, these metrics could be as follows: daily/weekly sales, weekly cash flow, backlog report, on-time shipments, returned items, gross profit margins, line of credit balance, production numbers, accounts over 60 days, etc.

Do yourself a tremendous favor. Hire a terrific Chief Financial Officer or Controller to manage your accounting and financial matters. Make sure this person knows how to gather, interpret, and explain financial data in simple terms. Be sure that she is proactive in her advice to you and focused on the future, not merely past performance. Also, make sure you have a top-notch CPA, banker, insurance professional and financial planner as part of your adviser team. Sharp advisers that understand the issues a business owner faces are worth their weight in gold. Do not cut corners here. Hire the best and their value and benefit will far exceed their cost.

Suggested Action Items:

- Leadership means everything to the success of your business and personal life. True leaders create clarity of direction, priorities, and expectations. To grow your business, freedom and fulfillment, you must grow your leadership capacity.
- Rate your leadership effectiveness on a scale of 1-10 (10 being the highest). Also, try to pinpoint your specific leadership areas to improve. Share these evaluations with your coach and other key advisers. Have them hold you accountable for growing as a leader.
- Buy biographies, tapes, or CDs on three great leaders you admire (CEOs, coaches, or political/religious/cause-oriented leaders) and model their philosophies, mindsets and strategies.
- Admit to yourself and your coach that you are 100% responsible for the results and condition of your business. No more excuses!
- Schedule a month in which to tackle vision creation for your business. For the first two weeks, act like a Chief Listening Officer. Get input from all your internal and external stakeholders (employees, customers, CPA, banker, attorney, consultants, suppliers, vendors, investors, etc.). Have them share their thoughts about your company's SWOTs (strengths, weaknesses, opportunities, and threats).
- After listening to what others have said, it's time to listen to your gut and heart. Spend a few days in your "CEO Cave" digesting the input from others, industry trends, competitive positions, and your thoughts on your company's SWOTs. Launch your vision from a platform of reality. However,

create a powerful vision (crusade) that engages the hearts, souls, minds, bodies and imaginations of your employees.

- Once you create your vision for the company, start "selling" the vision to all your internal and external stakeholders. You are now the Chief Enthusiasm Officer or Chief Storytelling Officer. Share the vivid and exciting details of how the business will look in 1, 3 and 5 years.

- If you are not an effective storyteller, have your coach or another adviser work with you. While you don't need to be a dynamic or charismatic leader, you need to be able to sell your vision effectively (tell the business story). Take speaking lessons if necessary. Also, be aware that your actions and where you spend your time and resources send a stronger message than your words. Relative to your vision, have your words and actions in alignment.

- You must drive the focus in your company on What's Important Now (WIN). Make sure your team is doing the right things, not merely things right. With the help of your coach and key managers, be sure to focus your team on six primary areas:

  - **Exceeding the expectations of your customers** You are in business to attract, serve, delight and retain customers in a profitable manner.

  - **Valuing results, not tolerating excuses** – Establish a goal-oriented culture with solid expectations of intelligent action and meaningful results.

  - **Continuous improvement** – "Good enough never is" ... drive out fear and allow your employees to experiment like crazy on new ideas, concepts and approaches. Test new ideas and keep the ones that work better than existing approaches. Conduct one-hour business improvement workshops every week. For every good idea worth pursuing, assign a champion, due date and key steps. Monitor progress and insist on aggressive implementation and follow-through.

- **Achieving profitable growth** – Don't focus just on revenues, focus on profits. Cut costs and grow profitable revenues. Engage the best CPA you can afford.
- **Maintaining a long-term perspective** – Do not take shortcuts and always do what is right. Repeat business is the life force of your company. Know the Lifetime Value of your customers.
- **Having fun** – Celebrate often, praise often, have fun.

- Be bold and decisive. Practice making decisions (based on the known facts) quickly, and change your mind, if at all, slowly.
- Learn to delegate. Learn to trust your people and systems. If a task isn't your area of brilliance, delegate. If someone else can do the task 80% as well as you can, give it up – delegate. Or ask, "Is this task worth $200 per hour?" If not, find someone else internally or externally to do this task.
- Ask your coach to help you with delegation.
- Face reality. See your company without any delusions or blind spots. See the way things really are, not what they were or what you wish them to be. Always have a fix on your company's SWOTs.
- Learn to share knowledge and seek fresh ideas:
    - Tap into everyone's brainpower. Ask internal and external contacts to pretend to be CEO of your company for a day and give ideas to improve profits, sales, operations, products/services, customer satisfaction, team spirit, etc.

- Join a CEO peer group to exchange ideas, challenges, solutions, and fresh approaches. Look beyond your industry for ideas and solutions.
- If you haven't done so, form a Board of outside advisers that will share their diversity, experiences, objectivity and ideas with you.
- Get a handle on your company's financial numbers. Learn about basic accounting concepts and financial reports. Have your CPA create "dashboard metrics".
- Hire a proactive and top-notch Chief Financial Officer, Controller or Accounting Manager for your business. Someone who can gather, interpret and explain financial results and trends. Hire the best CPA you can afford.

CLARITY OF DIRECTION: A SIMPLE BUSINESS PLAN

Points to Ponder

- *Let our advance worrying become advance thinking and planning.*

  Winston Churchill

- *Planning is bringing the future into the present so that you can do something about it now.*

  Alan Lakein

- *A good plan is like a road map: it shows the final destination and usually marks the best way to get there.*

  H. Stanley Judd

- *The best plans are straightforward documents that spell out the who, what, where, why and how much.*

  Paula Nelson

- *Our goals can only be reached through a vehicle of a plan, in which we must fervently believe, and upon which we must vigorously act. There is no other route to success.*

  Stephen A. Brennen

Keep Business Simple

To be an effective CEO, you must adopt a big-picture perspective. As leader, don't over complicate business. Keep it simple and straightforward. Simplicity allows for clarity of focus and focus allows for superior performance. Here is a simple framework by which to see and guide your enterprise.

As owner or CEO, you are solely responsible for the company's leadership process (direction, strategy, focus, goals, accountability)

and the business development process (building a systems-based business that is self-managing, self-improving, and nearly runs itself). As such, there are only a handful of additional major processes you need to ensure are in place, well documented, and working smoothly and optimally: marketing, selling, operations (customer fulfillment), customer service, and back-office functions.

In brief, the marketing process generates leads, the selling process generates customers by closing leads, and the operations process fulfills the promises made to the customer. Completing the business cycle is the customer service process that follows up with the customer to ensure satisfaction with the current transaction and to uncover any other unmet needs.

Since the purpose of any business is to find, satisfy and keep customers, marketing, selling, operations, and customer service processes should be your top priorities and areas of focus. Other functions, while important, should be secondary priorities and support this main mission. These back-office support functions are: a finance/accounting process to manage money; human resources to manage employee issues; and infrastructure to manage technology, facilities, administration, etc.

Spend your time and energy focusing on your company's core processes and competencies – those functions that you do extremely well as an organization and which add real value to the customer. Keeping business simple will help you stay focused on what is most important.

To simplify your business and your life even more, consider outsourcing (turning over day-to-day responsibility to an outside provider) your back-office functions such as payroll processing, tax preparation, legal, HR, technology, facilities management, etc. Seek advice from your CPA, attorney, or banker about outsourcing arrangements.

Planning for Results

How do you create a simple business plan? How do you achieve results? Again, you must keep things simple and focused. With your team's involvement, agree on and set annual goals. Then, on a 90-day cycle, gather your team and hold your people accountable for the agreed-upon results. This implementation process is just as important as the goals. Do not tolerate excuses; insist on execution and results.

In short, you must select a few key strategies and implement like mad. Success is more about execution than anything else. Focus on the vital few instead of the trivial many. Energy focused on a few highly important goals is powerful.

Please note that we are not talking about setting goals to achieve incremental improvements in performance or processes. We are talking about big and bold goals – goals on steroids. Be innovative and think big. Go for breakthroughs, not mere incremental gains. Realize there are no rules or restrictions. As long as what you do is moral, legal, and ethical, do not be shackled by company history or industry standards or practices. In short, kill the "we have always done it this way" mentality. Shake habitual thinking patterns.

Performance goals, at a minimum, should be set in the critical success areas we just discussed: leadership, business systemization, marketing, selling, operations (fulfillment), customer service, and back-office operations. In fact, your annual business plan could be nothing more than 3-5 monster-size goals in each one of these key areas. Once you have your annual goals established, assign a person to champion each cause. Give each person the authority, time, and tools to make things happen. On a 90-day cycle, hold each person accountable for progress on his or her goal(s).

These audacious, challenging, and adrenalin-inducing goals should be SMART (**S**pecific, **M**easurable, **A**chievable, **R**eally Desired, and **T**imed). Force your people to stretch. What gets measured gets done. What gets rewarded gets repeated. As a leader, insist on aggressive implementation, follow-up, follow-through, and results. Intentions and plans are mostly meaningless; implementation is where success is found.

Hire a Retreat Facilitator

If necessary, consider having a once-a-year off-site strategic retreat with your management team and/or key players. I strongly encourage hiring an objective facilitator to make sure there is honest dialogue, everyone participates, all the key barriers and issues are addressed, buy-in is achieved, and a workable action plan emerges. In the end, each person should know the answers to:

- Where are we going? (clarity of direction)
- What's expected of me? (my contribution)
- How will I be measured (accountability)
- How will I benefit? (rewards)

Before the retreat, this facilitator should interview each of your managers and/or key employees on a one-to-one basis to get an honest lay of the land. The facilitator will gain critical feedback and advice by asking the following types of questions:

- Please share with me thoughts about your company's:
  - Strengths
  - Weaknesses/Areas to improve
  - Opportunities
  - Threats
  - Competitive landscape
  - What makes us unique, different, valuable

82

- Your management team's:
    - Strengths/Weaknesses/Opportunities/Threats
    - Ability to handle growth
    - Ability to lead
    - Ability to delegate

- Please share with me thoughts about your personal:
    - Strengths/Weaknesses
    - Role/responsibilities
    - Ability to lead
    - Ability to delegate
    - Expectations for the strategic retreat

- If you were made CEO:
    - What changes would you make?
    - How would you dramatically improve our revenues?
    - How would you dramatically improve our operations?
    - How would you dramatically improve our value to customers?
    - What people would you dismiss?
    - What people would you cultivate to lead?

- On a scale of 1-10 (10 being highest), how would you rate the company's performance in each of these areas:
    - Sales
    - Marketing
    - Operations (customer fulfillment)
    - Leadership (clarity of vision, direction, objectives, accountability)
    - Business processes
    - Customer service

- Back-office functions (accounting, finance, HR, technology, etc.)
- Our people

- On a scale of 1-10 (10 being highest), how clear is the company's current:
    - Vision/Direction/Focus
    - Goals
    - Strategies
    - Accountability process
    - Review and compensation process

- On a scale of 1-10 (10 being highest), how clear is/are your:
    - Role(s)
    - Contributions
    - Responsibilities

Armed with this critical knowledge, your facilitator should be able to ensure a productive retreat that improves the performance of your people and company.

Also, strongly consider hiring the facilitator or a coach to come back on a monthly basis to ensure that the business plan is being properly implemented. This person can help hold your company and team accountable for taking action.

Suggested Action Items:

- Keep business simple.
- Set annual and 90-day goals in the critical success areas: leadership, business systems, marketing, sales, operations (customer fulfillment), customer service, and back-office functions.

- Conduct a strategic retreat at least once-a-year at an off-site facility.
- Strongly consider hiring a facilitator to do pre-interviews, orchestrate the retreat, and help with post-retreat implementation.

PEOPLE MANAGEMENT

Points to Ponder

- *Coming together is a beginning; keeping together is progress; working together is success.*

  Henry Ford
- *It doesn't make much difference how much other knowledge or experience an executive possesses; if he is unable to achieve results through people, he is worthless as an executive.*

  J. Paul Getty
- *There is no such thing as a self-made man. You will reach your goals only with the help of others.*

  George Shinn
- *If you don't know where you are going, how can you expect to get there?*

  Basil S. Walsh
- *People with goals succeed because they know where they're going.*

  Earl Nightingale

Many relevant people management topics were already addressed in the chapters on leadership and business planning. As you will recall, we covered such relevant people management topics as:

- Leadership basics
- Being 100% responsible as the owner
- Creating and articulating a vision
- Focusing your team on customers, results, innovation, profits, a long-term horizon and having fun
- Avoiding micro-management
- Delegating

- Being bold and decisive
- Facing reality
- Sharing knowledge
- Keeping business simple
- Creating a simple business plan
- Setting and achieving 90-day goals

In this chapter, we will focus on the critical importance of getting the right people on the ship, how to keep them accountable, how to establish trust with your team, and how everything you do contributes to the culture of your company.

Your Greatest Asset

You cannot reach your vision and goals without the help of others. Your greatest asset is people – the "right" people. People that share your company's values, ethics, personality, culture and vision. Your primary objective is to get the right people on your ship, the wrong people off, and then direct the course of the ship yourself. Therefore, recruiting, training/coaching, developing and retaining your competent employees are critical success factors for your company, and some of your top responsibilities as a leader. Your focus should be to develop others and create the right conditions for their success. In short, unleash the full human potential of your organization.

What Employees Want

Here is an unscientific crash course in what employees want:

- To know where the company is headed and why
- To know their roles, responsibilities and what is expected of them
- To know how they will be evaluated and rewarded

- To utilize their talents in the best way possible
- To feel appreciated and valued – that their work and ideas matter
- To be coached – challenged, motivated and held accountable
- To have the right tools, training and authority to do their jobs
- To contribute in a meaningful way to the company and its mission
- To grow and develop – to reach their potential
- To have an emotionally connected, competent leader of character support their success

Hiring/Firing Basics

Hire for talent, not just resume data. Be sure to hire emotionally engaged people, people with passion in their eyes and fire in the belly. Match their talent to the position – again, help them to be successful. Don't hesitate to use personal assessment tests to better understand the aptitudes, attitudes and talents of potential employees.

While you should hire people slowly, fire them quickly if they do not fit your culture and can't operate within your system. Do not let emotionally disengaged people or negative people infect your company. Do not waste time and energy trying to rehabilitate poor performers (the lower 20% that cause 80% of your headaches). Spend your time and effort with your top performers, the top 20%. This top 20% will produce 80% of your company's results. Therefore, put tremendous effort into developing and retaining the right people. For your business to grow, you must find and develop the right people.

Because you cannot control everything, the development of your system and your people is paramount. Spend time and effort hiring the right people to manage your system. Hire excellent leaders and managers. Then let your managers hire competent employees (not necessarily brilliant ones) to work the system. They should hire hard working and loyal people who will follow the system and execute their duties according to documented practices. Again, hire emotionally engaged people with passion in their souls. Their focus should be on working the system and improving the operations manual, as necessary. They should not be free-lancing, improvising or winging it.

Developing Your People

True leaders care about their people and their on-the-job education and development. Make sure you have a fair, annual performance review process in place. Employees crave feedback on how they are performing. When it comes to your employees, view yourself as an educator and developer of people. Make sure they know your system as well as your expectations for their roles and responsibilities within it. Continually share your vision with them and your guiding principles. Clarity of purpose is critical to employees. Give them a defined structure, order, sense of purpose and meaning. In short, take care of the team; the team will take care of your customers and business.

Also, make certain your employees understand bottom-line fundamentals and how they can contribute to improved profits. They need to know how their daily thoughts, actions, and inactions impact profits and customer satisfaction. Let them feel a real sense of responsibility for profits and clients. Furthermore, let them know you expect them to continually share new ways to grow revenues, eliminate inefficiencies, and improve business practices. Most employees will try to live up to your expectations.

As leader, you should be developing future leaders in your organization. You gain tremendous leverage by developing the leadership skills of your people. This leadership development effort also helps with crisis management events, succession planning, and eventually selling the business. As such, focus more time, energy, and effort on taking care of your best performers and much less time on your trouble employees. The more leaders you develop, the greater impact they will have throughout the organization. To stop working in your business, you need to hand over daily reins to competent leaders.

You can also leverage past employees. Keep track of where your prior employees have gone. They are your alumni. If they left on good terms, keep in touch and maintain some form of on-going communication. They can feed you future employees, customers, and who knows, they may rejoin your organization themselves.

Keep Your People Accountable

Too many leaders do not hold their people accountable for reaching established goals or performance standards. In my opinion, such lack of accountability is one of the deadly business mistakes.

What's currently happening in most small businesses? Meetings are held, issues are discussed, solutions are proposed, and goals are set. Unfortunately, the story usually ends there. Implementation is weak at best. Follow-up is missing. Follow-through is missing. Accountability is missing. Ideas, strategies, and tactics never get off the ground. Many promises fall through the cracks. What a waste of time and talent.

Why does this mistake happen? Owners are not functioning as leaders. They are not monitoring progress on goals. They are too busy in the details of the business to focus on the performance of others or the overall performance of the company.

Moreover, too many business owners try to be liked instead of respected. Holding people accountable can be confrontational at times. Many owners avoid tension, conflict, and on-going performance reviews. Such avoidance is dangerous to your business and the development of your people. Don't be everyone's buddy. Don't try to be popular. This isn't high school. As a leader, you need to be respected, not necessarily liked. Above all else, you are their boss and a challenging coach that demands the best of each player.

Meet with your key employees or managers at least once a month for a one-to-one, good-old-fashioned accountability session. Remind them of your expectations. Help them to grow and improve. Again, when you create clarity of expectations and standards, there is less confusion and more effective delegation and accountability.

Be very careful about letting your employees become your social friends. You need to remain objective to make decisions in the best interest of the company. If you want a friend, get a pet. If you want to be liked by everyone, sell your business and get a job. Trying to please or be liked by everyone is a sure bet for disaster.

Give people the responsibility, freedom, resources, and support required to get important things done. Let them know they will be held accountable for certain results. Continually remind them of your expectations. Monitor their progress and intervene only when necessary. Give them feedback. Praise an employee's progress on goals in public and criticize their poor performance in private. However, in public, feel free to express your disappointment and frustration to your entire team. Just save the harsh criticism for an individual for behind closed doors. Praise in public; criticize in private.

Here are some basic ground rules for effective accountability:
- Never let committees, groups or multiple persons be accountable for making things happen.
- Make sure one person/one champion is responsible and accountable for each key assignment.

- Establish goals and clarify due dates for results.
- Conduct regularly scheduled follow-up meetings to gauge progress on goals and hold people accountable.
- If they consistently fail to get important things done, give them different jobs or replace them with new people.

Do not allow poor implementation to infect your business. It's a cancer, a death sentence. You have only two choices; you can establish a culture that tolerates excuses or one that insists on performance. Do you want more excuses or execution of goals? For improved results, you must start leading and holding your people accountable.

People want to be held accountable and challenged. They also want constant feedback on their performance. They want to learn and to grow. They even desire a healthy environment of discipline. All this helps them develop and reach their potential. Accountability is beneficial feedback that shows you care. Make certain your employees feel appreciated and important – they crave it!

As CEO, who will hold you accountable? Again, get a coach or use a Board of Advisers. Such people will help you reach your greater potential.

Trust or Bust

Trust is the fabric that holds a company together. If people do not trust you, they will not trust your vision or strategies. You are doomed. If you lose your character and reputation, you will have lost everything. Here are some suggestions:
- Do what you say you will do. Let them count on you. Keep your promises.
- In good times and bad, be ethical, moral, trustworthy, and possess unquestioned integrity.

- Your words and actions must be in alignment. Walk the talk. Be a straight shooter.
- Honesty is paramount.
- You must lead by example.
- Be an authentic person – what people see is who you are.
- You must share the good, the bad, and the neutral news with your team. Open communication is a must.
- No employee will complain about being kept too informed, too involved, or too inspired.
- Be sincere and always speak from the heart -- phonies are easy to spot.
- Build trust with deep listening.

Trust must be earned over time. However, trust can be lost in no time and is very difficult to rebuild, if at all. As such, any untrustworthy behavior will cost you good employees. Good employees do not leave bad companies; they leave bad leaders.

Culture Creation

As leader, know that you set the tone, pace, environment, and personality of your company. By your consistent actions, you establish what the company values and what gets rewarded. You lead by example and to a large extent, shape the culture of your organization.

In large part, you maintain the culture by participating in the interviewing, hiring, reviewing and rewarding of your employees. Always make time for these critical activities.

Above all, try to create a culture where your people feel appreciated and important, and where they can fully use their talents and reach their potential. William James said that "the deepest principle in human nature is the craving to be appreciated." If you achieve such a supportive and fear-free culture, you will have created a successful company with solid retention of your employees.

Also, make coming to work enjoyable. Identify, celebrate, and remember your company's victories. Capture them in stories that you repeat, especially to new hires.

Suggested Action Items:

- Your greatest asset is finding, hiring, developing and retaining the "right" people for your company. Get the right people on the ship, the wrong people off the ship, and the ship heading in the right direction.
- Spend time taking care of your best performers, not your worst performers. Spend time developing future leaders – you will gain tremendous leverage.
- Leverage past employees. Keep in touch with your alumni. They can feed you new customers and new employees.
- Keep your people accountable. Do not try to be everyone's buddy. You must insist on performance. Be sure to have a performance review process in place that evaluates the contribution of every team member once or twice a year.
- Be sure you have an on-going accountability process in place for your key goals. Conduct weekly accountability sessions to gauge progress on goals. Insist on performance; do not tolerate excuses.
- Trust is everything. If your employees don't trust you, they will not follow you. Keep your promises and do what you say you will do. Walk the talk. Share good news, bad news and neutral news. Trust your employees and they will trust you.
- You set the tone, pace and climate of your business. Create a culture where your employees feel appreciated, important and capable of reaching their full potential.

MASTERING THE POWER OF MARKETING

Points to Ponder

- *The greatest mistake a person can make is to be afraid of making one.*
  Elbert Hubbard
- *Failure is only the opportunity to more intelligently begin again.*
  Henry Ford
- *An idea is the only lever which moves the world.*
  Arthur F. Covey
- *I use not only all the brains I have, but also all I can borrow.*
  Woodrow Wilson
- *Ideas are the beginning points of all fortunes.*
  Napoleon Hill
- *If you want to succeed, double your failure rate.*
  Thomas Watson
- *Because its purpose is to create a customer, the business has two – and only two – functions: marketing and innovation. Marketing and innovation produce results. All the rest are costs.*
  Peter Drucker
- *There's a way to do it better... find it.*
  Thomas Edison

Worth repeating, the purpose of every business is to find, satisfy and retain customers in a profitable manner. The real value of your business is directly tied to the future, predictable cash flow from your customers/clients. Marketing will help you achieve this critical imperative by growing geometrically instead of incrementally. A strategic business owner takes full advantage of the power and leverage of marketing.

Growing Your Business

What is marketing? First, it's about understanding deeply the needs and wants of your customers and providing them with greater value. You must clearly identify the demand in the marketplace. At a minimum, most businesses can improve significantly in this area. However, the real power and leverage of marketing comes from the next level of influence, communicating convincingly your unique and superior value proposition.

Marketing is about communicating with and educating your customers, prospects, and referral sources why it's in their best interest to do business with your company. It is about educating the right target audience on the unique and superior advantages, benefits, value, and results you can provide and sharing the credible evidence/reasons that support and back-up such promises. In short, marketing is about educating your target market on the advantages of doing business with you and the reasons why they should trust you to deliver on your promises.

Instead of impacting one prospect at a time (i.e. direct selling), marketing allows you to communicate with, educate, and influence many buyers at once. In a sense, marketing is a one-to-many selling system. Marketing allows you to target and influence large groups of customers, prospects, alliances, referral sources, reporters, etc. in a single action.

Unfortunately, most business owners mistakenly try to tackle most goals (i.e. growing sales) with a one-to-one, single weapon, combat mentality. For example, instead of considering the leverage of marketing (i.e. strategic alliances, referral systems, direct mail, telemarketing, etc.) to grow sales, many owners remain in the same comfort zone and deadly rut of using a single weapon like direct selling. They miss the chance to use air support (marketing) to vastly aid their ground war (selling). They fail to consider and try new options, new approaches, and new strategies.

While all businesses have a selling process (converting leads to customers), most do not have a legitimate marketing process (generating qualified leads). As such, they miss out on tremendous leverage and opportunities.

Your goal should be to add an on-going marketing process to your business. Again, marketing is nothing more than understanding the needs of your customers and then communicating to them the superior advantages/benefits they can derive by doing business with you. Think of marketing as on-going education. You are educating customers, prospects, and referral sources why it's in their best interest to do business with your company.

There are only 5 ways to grow your business:
        1) Keep the customers you have,
        2) Bring in more customers,
        3) Increase the average transaction size (unit sale),
        4) Increase the frequency of purchases, and
        5) Say "no" to bad customers/prospects.

In short, keep what you have, bring in more customers, sell larger amounts to them, and sell to them more often. Do one or more of these and your business grows. Do two or more of these well and your business can grow by quantum leaps and bounds -- geometric growth instead of mere linear growth.

Keep What You Have, Grow What You Have

Don't under estimate the need to satisfy and retain customers. Most businesses put too much money, time, and effort into chasing new customers/prospects and far too little resources trying to keep their current ones. However, we all know that you can't fill up a bucket if you don't plug the current leaks. Real profits and stable revenue streams come from long-term relationships and repeat business with your current, loyal, profitable customers. Some experts declare that 80% of a company's future growth comes from existing clients, if served and cultivated properly. As such, customer satisfaction and retention should be your #1 marketing priority.

Again, the purpose of a business is to attract and retain customers. You can't grow and remain in business without keeping the customers you currently have. First, you must measure your current attrition rate (loss of customers) and set a goal for dramatically reducing this rate. For example, let's say, on average, that you lose 20% of your customers every year. A realistic goal would be to reduce this attrition rate to 10% per year. Bottom line, it is easier and nearly eight times cheaper to serve and retain current clients/customers than to pursue new ones.

Once you have plugged the holes in your attrition bucket, you want to serve better and get closer to these profitable and worthy customers. You want to better understand their needs and then fulfill as many of these needs as possible with additional products and services. Continually communicate with your customers. Give them value. Give them solutions. Focus on them and their needs, not on your products/services.

Communicate with them in person, in letters, in faxes, in emails, via your website, brief newsletters, etc. Don't worry, you can't over-communicate with your customers. Like employees, keep them informed, involved, and inspired to continue doing business with you. Also, repeatedly ask your customers the following questions:

- "How are we doing?"
- "What other needs do you have?" and
- "How could we improve our value to you?"

Your objective is to provide them with more value more frequently and as a result, you will benefit with more profits. Never sell a customer only once. Real profits come from repeat business. As such, set goals to increase the frequency and size of repeat business. You want on-going relationships and on-going sales.

Winning New Customers and Clients

Bottom line, to be successful at winning new customers and clients, you need to be perceived as being different, special, better. You cannot afford to be viewed as a commodity. Commodity companies are paid commodity prices and fees. There is tremendous power and profits in being perceived as unique, different, better.

Spend time researching and establishing your company's Unique Selling Proposition (USP). What is your most powerful, compelling benefit or advantage? What is the big, overt advantage of your product or service? Why do customers continue to do business with you? What major frustrations do you remove from their lives? Once you define your USP, broadcast it like mad in your sales presentations, in your brochures, in your direct mail, on your website, in your telephone answering methods, in your advertisements, in your news releases, etc.

Do not let your USP simply be *quality, service, and price.* This says nothing different and has no emotional power. It sounds trite and comes across as "blah, blah, blah" to your prospective customers. Instead, clearly delineate your differences and performance guarantees. Instead of being a mere marketing consultant, be a marketing partner that guarantees revenue results (pay-for-performance) or the client doesn't pay. Now that is different and understandable. FedEx's earlier USP was "when it positively, absolutely needs to be there overnight".

Additionally, to achieve substantial increases in profits and customer satisfaction, you must challenge yourself to come up with new products and services or repackage old ones in a way that truly excites and delights customers and clients. To qualify as killer ideas and killer solutions, they need to include the following:

1) An obvious, compelling **benefit** to the potential buyer
2) Believable **evidence or reasons** that support this benefit (credibility)
3) **A significant difference** from existing products or services (dramatically new and better) and,
4) A simple and effective means to communicate the benefit, evidence, and difference to the target market.

Such killer ideas can revolutionize your business and industry. Dream big.

In addition to being perceived as different, special and better, you need to try new marketing strategies to attract new customers and clients. Here are some other brief ideas for bringing in new clients:

- **Leverage your past customer relationships.** Revisit with past, worthy customers or inactive customers and express your interest in re-kindling the relationship and solving any of their current problems. These folks did business with you at one time, wrote out checks to you, and may well be receptive to re-activating their relationship with you. However, you must identify and heal any unresolved wounds and share with them the benefits of doing business with your company once again. Give them an inducement (bonus, discount, additional service level, etc.) for taking action and ordering once again.

- **Formalize and optimize your referral systems.** Identify (crunch numbers, don't rely on hunches) your best-performing referral sources (some use the term market influencers) over the past 12 months and be sure that you thank and reward them for their efforts. Communicate with these proven providers often to maintain a top-of-mind awareness. Once you identify these top providers, shamelessly clone these folks. For example, if you are a house painting company and determine that your best referral sources have been real estate agents, replicate this formula. Don't complicate the magic. Educate these and others as to the specific types of customers and circumstances you serve best. Referral source cultivation is one of the most underutilized yet low-cost, high-yield marketing weapons that exist.

- **Leverage those relationships that your business helps to financially support** (your banker, CPA, attorney, suppliers, financial adviser, insurance agent, etc.). To determine which would make for good informal sales agents for your business, ask the following types of questions: "Who will benefit from our success as we continue to grow and expand?" "Who do we write checks to on a regular basis and would have a vested interest in supporting our business development efforts?" Identify these relationships and ask these folks to reciprocate and support your growth efforts through leads, referrals, testimonials, etc.

- **Leverage indirect competitors to gain new customers.** Indirect competitors are companies that you seldom go head-to-head with competing for business. For example, you could establish a formal referral relationship (swap leads, pay finder's fees, share revenue, co-marketing, etc.) with an indirect competitor that is much larger or smaller than you are or in a different geographic region. For example, a smaller CPA firm could establish an alliance with a large CPA firm and swap leads that don't fit their respective niches. A small, traditional plumbing business could form an alliance with a plumbing company that focuses on doing only the tough, complex, big jobs. Leads could flow both ways.

- **Gain leverage from current clients and customers.** Ask current buyers for introductions and referrals to other potential buyers or ask current customers to provide endorsements, testimonials, or serve as references. Always ask current clients about other unmet needs they may have.

- **Identify and cultivate complementary businesses as strategic alliances**. For example, a technology consulting firm would want to form alliances with those that can help steer business their way (CPAs, software/hardware vendors, other non-competitive consultants, etc.) How do you find potential referral or alliance partners? Ask, "Who already has the trust and respect of our prospects?"

- **Make doing business easy, convenient, and risk free**. Do not ask the other party to assume risk if they start a business relationship with you. Instead, communicate an unconditional, money-back guarantee. Don't keep your guarantee hidden, broadcast it. A credible and specific guarantee will bring in far more business than it costs you. Here is a simple example, "If you don't find our technology training courses among the best you have ever taken, simply ask for a refund before the start of the second day and we will gladly return 100% of your money without any questions or delay."

- **Use direct-response advertising.** Don't waste money on ineffective advertising. Always make sure any advertising contains a compelling offer or benefit and motivates the reader, listener, or viewer to take action. Never advertise just an image. Advertise only to sell something. Track the effectiveness of your ads to generate leads and/or sales. If the ads don't seem to be working, kill them. Never advertise to merely satisfy your ego.

- **Consider using telemarketing.** Use it to develop leads for your salespeople or use telemarketers to follow-up a direct mail or advertising campaign. Even consider using telemarketing to follow up a sale to see if the person requires any additional help, advice, services or products (warranties, add-on products, additional levels of service, etc.) If you just cleaned the carpet in two rooms of a customer's house, call up a week later and ask if they would want additional rooms to look as good and offer them a discount as inducement for taking immediate action.

- **Influence many people at once with special events/seminars.** Consider hosting educational events for customers, referral sources, and prospects. Consider holding them in conjunction with other companies (newspapers, radio stations, suppliers, banks, CPA firms, industry experts, trade associations, complementary companies, etc.). This will allow you to tap into their customer relationships. For example, if you are an upscale travel agency introducing new exotic trips, consider co-hosting an event with an upscale radio station, magazine or with a high-end jewelry store, auto dealership, country club, money management firm, etc.

- **Consider using direct mail.** Direct mail is simply putting a powerful and complete sales presentation in writing. Such a vehicle allows you to touch many buyers at once – immense leverage. Most owners would be best served in the long run by hiring a professional direct marketer on a project basis.

- **Consider using public relations.** Public relations can be a powerful source of leverage as you educate and influence a targeted audience about your benefits, expertise, etc. Get to know the reporters in your industry and periodically call them with some story ideas.

- **Gain leverage by improving the effectiveness of your sales approach.** Give your sales people a proven, simple sales methodology. For example, use READ. Relate to your prospect. Establish the Need or Problem. Advance a Tailored Solution. Determine Next Steps. It's all about building relationships and solving problems. Buy books, tapes, CDs on selling skills and distribute to your team. Also, periodically send your salespeople to strategic selling courses. Huge payoff!
- **Buy other reputable businesses** possessing great reputations and strong goodwill to gain access to their loyal customers. Be sure their business is a good fit for your company, culture, values, customer base, etc.

Increase the Amount/Frequency of Purchases

To be successful at getting your current customers to spend more with your organization and more often, you must increase the "perceived value" of what you offer. You must educate your customers so that they desire your products and services even more.

To make this happen, you must first increase the collective "self-esteem" of your organization. You and your employees must believe that you are different, better, special and highly valuable to your customers, even worth a premium price. You must fight the "we are a commodity" mindset with every fiber of your mind, body, and soul. The day you believe you are in a commodity industry or business is the day you begin to die. If you are similar to the others, you must break out from the pack. For example, add more services to your offering, give greater performance and money-back guarantees, provide on-going education seminars for your buyers or consider packaging or bundling other products or services with yours. Again, be different and more valuable.

Here are some ideas to increase the average purchase size and frequency of your sales:

- **Raise your prices, if you can**. Educate your buyers on the superior advantages, benefits and results you provide them and explain "the reasons why" you need to raise prices – increasing manufacturing costs, customer-service enhancements, better guarantees, better ingredients, etc.

- **Upsell**. If your client/customer can achieve better results and more satisfaction, educate them on buying a higher-end product or service. Do a better job of assessing their needs and matching to products or services that will give them the optimal buying experience and satisfaction. You will increase your profits and their fulfillment. Auto dealers are masters at getting customers to buy car models with the higher-end feature packages (i.e. leather interior, better stereos, etc.)

- **Cross-sell.** If you have multiple product lines or service lines, communicate and educate your customers and clients on the full spectrum of your solutions -- services, products, and expertise. Continually ascertain their challenges and problems and match up with the other solutions you offer. CPA firms, for example, cross-sell their audit clients on tax and consulting services. Banks cross-sell their checking customers on investments, mortgages, lines of credit, credit cards, etc.

- **Bundle better**. Consider packaging complementary products and services together. If a customer is going to buy a gas grill, for example, offer them a complete package of cooking utensils, mesquite wood chips, barbecue book, grill cover and apron. By saving the customer time and helping them to buy a more "complete solution", you can probably charge a premium for this "barbecue in the box" offering. At the very least, they will have bought more than they otherwise would have – you made buying easy.

- **Offer volume or frequent buyer discounts**. If you can get your customers to buy more and buy more frequently, reward them with incentives, discounts, extra level of services, etc. Since you have maximized your cash flow, be willing to reward them with a few extra perks. Bookstores and airlines have "frequent buyer" programs. For example, video stores and coffee stores give you a free serving when you buy a certain number of times.

- **Offer other products and services that will complement what you already sell.** Ask the question, "Who else sells something that goes before, after or along with my customer's purchase?" For example, if you sell computer products, consider selling "technical needs analysis" services on the front-end or installation and computer training services on the back-end. Be sure it makes economic sense to add such services to your business.

- **Communicate with your customers often and give them buying ideas or solutions via mail, phone, email, newsletters, in-store displays, etc**. For example, if you are a hardware store, and as early fall approaches, use direct mail and in-store displays to communicate to your customers the need to fill cracks and seal coat their driveways. Sell them on the benefits of taking such action. Package all the supplies together (sealant, crack filler, broom, gloves, removal cleaner, "how to" booklet, etc.) and offer a single-solution price.

- **Conduct special events to educate your existing customers on your additional service/product offerings.** Do this in an informative manner and in a way that has "their best interests" at heart. Hold a "sneak preview" for your new products, services, models, etc. Hold exclusive events for your best customers. An upscale luxury auto dealer might hold a wine and cheese party with a musical quartet to unveil the newest car models.

- **Endorse other people's products or services to your client list and get a cut of the action.** For example, if you are an upscale jewelry store, consider offering elaborate vacation packages to your customers via an upscale travel agency. Mail offers to your customer database, endorse the travel agency and their offering, and receive a set percentage of any revenues generated. Instead of adding computer training to your computer store, form an alliance with a reputable training company and negotiate for a "cut of the action" for introducing/endorsing them to your customers via email, direct mail, telemarketing, etc. To maintain the goodwill of your customers, make sure you do your "due diligence" and introduce only high-trust, high-integrity, high-value organizations to your customer base.

Selectively Say "NO"

Warning -- this section is advice aimed at those who sell primarily to businesses, not to walk-in, public customers.

To devote more time and attention to your best opportunities and customers, you need to adopt a selectivity mindset. You can't optimize your business performance if you are constantly bombarded by unprofitable, ungrateful, disagreeable, ever-complaining, and energy-draining customers. You and your employees deserve better.

You must learn to say no to prospects who do not fit your profitability profile and goodbye to cheap, unpleasant, unprofitable customers. This single act of firing your problem accounts frees up capacity so you can handle more profitable growth. The 80/20 rule (Pareto Principle) is a helpful guide. This rule says that 80% of your profits come from the top 20% of your customers. Conversely, 80% of your headaches and problems come from the lower 20% of your customer base (the dogs). It is these troublesome 20% that are draining your profits and life force. You need to wean them.

Either raise your prices to compensate for the pain and suffering they cause, or flat out fire them. That's right, have the courage to fire those customers that are a real burden to your people and organization. Since they are unprofitable, this will free up your people and resources to attract and win superior customers and provide more time, attention, and value to your existing quality customers. Your employees and your bottom-line will thank you.

As a suggestion, for those serving business entities, separate your customer base into "Tier 1", "Tier 2", and "Tier 3". Put most of your organization's time and talents into serving the heck out of Tier 1 customers. These are your most profitable customers that value, appreciate, and regularly buy your offerings. Spend slightly less resources on Tier 2 customers and provide minimal service to Tier 3 customers. Your goal is to develop Tier 2 to become Tier 1 accounts and move your Tier 3 customers up a rung or move them out the door.

Experiment Like Mad

No matter which strategies you employ, your ultimate leverage comes from focused brainpower -- intellectual capital and innovative ideas. Think "brain equity", not "sweat equity." One innovative idea could help your business achieve quantum breakthroughs in performance and results. One innovative idea could significantly multiply your leads generated, revenues, profits, customer satisfaction, level of quality or competitive advantage. As the leader, you need to encourage practical creativity, experimentation, and innovation – the process of asking better questions.

As a CEO, you should be experimenting with new approaches all the time. Have your employees test new strategies, hunches, sales approaches and marketing weapons. Small, controlled testing is critical if you are going to optimize your business and find incredible leverage points within and outside your business. For example, you could test the following:
- A new method of targeting your prospects
- A new sales presentation
- A new direct mail offer or special event

- A new headline in your ads, direct mail campaign, or press releases
- A new hiring or retention practice
- A new channel of distribution
- A new strategic alliance
- A new compensation structure
- A new collection method
- A new customer service initiative
- A new referral system
- A new internal communication method

Try many things and keep those that work better than existing approaches.

You need to listen continually to your employees, current and former customers, and team of advisors. Ask your internal and external contacts, "How can we improve _____ and get greater results?" If you think your ways or ideas are the best, all new ideas will pass you by. Look outside your industry as well for fresh ways and "killer" ideas. Do not be myopic. Be intellectually and emotionally curious and tuned into your employees, customers, and vendors, to name a few. Keep a small notebook, personal data assistant, or a recorder with you at all times to capture your ideas and make them your servants.

Suggested Action Items:

- Marketing is a weapon used by strategic business owners to achieve substantial growth. Commit to marketing. Commit resources.
- Marketing is about educating your target market (current and past customers, prospects, referral sources, influencers, etc.)

on the advantages of doing business with your company and the reasons why they should trust you to deliver on your promises. Make "education" and "influence" the focus of your marketing.

- Commit to add a robust marketing process (on-going education) to your business. Your goal is to educate and influence groups of people at a time.

- Remember this key concept: There are only 5 ways to grow your business: (1) keep the customers you have, (2) bring in more customers, (3) increase the average transaction size (unit sale), (4) increase the frequency of purchases, and (5) learn to say "no" to bad customers and prospects. In short, keep what you have, bring in more customers, sell larger amounts to them, and sell to them more often. Do one of these and your business grows. Do two or more well, and your business can grow by quantum leaps and bounds, geometric growth instead of mere linear growth.

- **Keep What You Have**.
    - Make customer and client retention your number one goal. Measure your current yearly attrition rate (loss of customers) and set a goal to reduce it in half.
    - Communicate with and continually educate your current customers on the advantages of your solutions. Use all means necessary: email, mail, phone, in-person, fax, brief newsletters, your website, etc. Learn to better understand their needs and ask them: (1)"how are we doing?" (2) "how could we improve our value to you?" and (3) "what other needs do you have?"

- **Attract New Customers**
    - Spend time crafting your Unique Selling Proposition (USP). What makes your business special, different and better? Communicate your competitive advantages like crazy in all you do and say.

- Come up with killer ideas for your products and services. Remember, to qualify as "killer ideas" and "killer solutions", they need to include the following: (1) an obvious, compelling **benefit** to the potential buyer (2) believable **evidence or reasons** that support this benefit (credibility) (3) **a significant difference** from existing products and services (dramatically new and better) and, (4) a simple and effective means to communicate the benefit, evidence, and difference to the target market. Such killer ideas can revolutionize your business and industry. Dream big.
- Consider trying 3-5 of these marketing strategies to gain new customers:
  - Leverage past customer relationships
  - Formalize and optimize your referral systems
  - Leverage those relationships that your business helps to financially support (CPAs, bankers, suppliers, etc.)
  - Leverage indirect competitors
  - Gain leads and referrals from current customers and clients
  - Identify and cultivate complementary businesses as strategic alliances
  - Make doing business with you easy, convenient, fun and risk free
  - Only use direct-response advertising, not image advertising
  - Consider the utilization of telemarketing
  - Use special events/seminars to influence groups of people
  - Consider using direct marketing
  - Consider public relations

- Improve the effectiveness of your company's sales approach/process
- Buy out other reputable and complementary businesses to gain their clients

- **Get Customers to Increase the Amount & Frequency of Purchases by implementing 3-5 of these strategies:**
  - Increase the collective "self-esteem" of your organization – fight the "we are a commodity" mindset
  - Raise your prices and explain why
  - Upsell
  - Cross-sell
  - Bundle your solutions (products & services) better
  - Offer volume or frequent buyer incentives
  - Offer other products/services that will complement what you currently sell
  - Communicate with your customers often and give them "opportunities" to buy
  - Conduct special events to educate current customers on your additional offerings
  - Endorse other people's products/services to your clients for a cut of the action

- **Learn to say "no" to unprofitable customers/prospects:**
  - Learn to say no to unworthy prospects and unprofitable customers. Fire your "dog" accounts. Use the 80/20 rule as a guide
  - Consider separating customers into a Tier System. Put most of your time and effort into serving your Tier 1 and Tier 2 accounts. Move Tier 3 up the rung or out the door

- **Experiment Like Mad**
  - As CEO, make sure your employees are continually asking questions like "how can we improve _____ and get better results?"
  - Test current marketing strategies and approaches against new ones. Keep those that work better, lose those that don't
  - Encourage experimentation – drive out fear
  - Look outside your business and industry for better ways to do things

STRATEGIC RELEASE-LEARNING TO LET GO

Points to Ponder

- *You never achieve real success unless you like what you are doing.*

  Dale Carnegie

- *To be what we are, and to become what we are capable of becoming, is the only end of life.*

  Robert Louis Stevenson

- *There is only one success – to be able to spend your life in your own way.*

  Christopher Morley

- *The best things in life aren't things.*

  Raven

- *Success is getting what you want. Happiness is wanting what you get.*

  Hayden

- *He who knows enough is enough will always have enough.*

  Lao-Tzu

- *He is a wise man who does not grieve for the things which he has not, but rejoices for those which he has.*

  Epictetus

After the first few years of business ownership, reality starts to set in. For most owners, the initial joy of "doing your own thing" has most likely faded. Your supposed ticket to freedom has turned into a sentence of servitude. Your "baby" has become a "rotten kid". What was once a very exciting mission has turned into a daily chore and grind. Your one-time American Dream now seems to be an exaggerated fairytale incapable of being attained.

Just because you own a business does not mean you must forego a fulfilling and active personal life. Quite the contrary, your business should be a tool to help you get more life, not less. A business should free you up, not tie you down.

If you have implemented the strategic business owner concepts discussed (thinking and acting like a CEO; systematizing and documenting the business; leading, planning, managing your people, and marketing), then letting go of the day-to-day and hour-to-hour operations of the business should be doable.

You Are Not Your Business

In order to build a business that functions without you (systems dependent), you need to think of yourself as separate from the business. You are not your business and your business is not you. View your business as a means to an end, a tool to help you create more fulfillment, freedom, wealth and options.

To let go and escape the tyranny of the details, you cannot be emotionally welded to the business. You are a worthwhile human being with or without your business. Do not let your ego, self-worth and self-esteem be tied up with the business. The business is but one facet of your life. While it is an important component of your life, it is not the end all. It should not fully define who you are.

Your value and worth as a human being are separate from the value of your business. You must not take your business too seriously. Odds are, you are not curing cancer. While whatever you are doing is important, it is not more important than your family, your friends, your health, your faith, your fulfillment and your joy in life.

For example, the time, attention, and love you share with your spouse, family, kids or friends are much more important to them than your title, business, money, etc. While you can always make more money, you cannot make more time or replay life. You do not get another chance to be a spouse, parent, friend, etc. This is not a dress rehearsal. Get your priorities in order now!

Keep things in perspective. No matter how bad things get, never forget that you have options. You can walk away from the business, sell it to someone else, or hire a professional business manager (Chief Operating Officer) to handle the day-to-day issues. Worst case, you can always get a job! Such options should prevent you from ever feeling totally trapped by or dependent on your business.

Before you can satisfy your employees, customers, investors, and business partners, you must first satisfy yourself with the business. It must serve your needs and wants over the long haul. If you don't stay in the game long enough, you do no one any good. There should be joy in being a business owner. Learn to let go. Trust your business system and trust your people.

Acknowledge Death

Stop the delusions. You will not live forever. You are right now using up your life force. You are not in control. You are not God. Time is running out. You cannot save time, invest it or buy more of it. You can only "spend" it. How wisely are you spending up your life force?

Be brave and be aware of you own mortality. Face facts, you have a limited time on earth. By acknowledging eventual death, life becomes sweeter, more meaningful and more precious. By facing death head on, you are liberated to live life fully. Realizing that life is unmistakably finite, you make wiser choices, especially about how, where, and with whom you spend time.

Do a quick test. It's called the tombstone test. Draw a tombstone and include your birth date, a dash, and your best guess for a death date. Do the math. Determine the years you have left. Now ask yourself, "What do I want written on my tombstone?" "How do I want to be remembered?" "What's my legacy?" "What really matters most to me?" Odds are, you want to be remembered as a good spouse, parent, friend, provider, a person of good character, a caring leader, follower of your faith, or for making a certain contribution to society.

Does your present way of living match your desired epitaph? Any regrets? Are you leading the type of life you want to be remembered for? No one on his deathbed wishes he had worked more hours, earned more money, bought more things, etc. My suggestion, focus on your faith, family, friends and leaving a legacy.

Stop living life reactively, letting urgent yet unimportant matters dictate your days. Face death and live your remaining years the way you truly want to, based on what is most important to you. What do you want to do before you die?

All in the Family

For many of you, you are also struggling to balance running a business with raising a family and nurturing a marriage or significant relationship. As a result, you are exhausted from treading water in a sea of multiple responsibilities, obligations and expectations. Not surprising, divorce rates of entrepreneurs are very high. Beat the odds by talking to your spouse or significant other about your business, your highs and lows, dreams, fears, challenges and feelings. Don't build a business yet destroy a marriage or key relationship. Stop being a lone ranger. Stop suffering in a silent shroud of secrecy. Again, share this book and your feelings with your spouse or significant other. Let them better understand your situation so that they can help you, support you, and challenge you.

While on the subject of relationships, be sure to schedule one-on-one time with your family members each week and schedule dates with your spouse/significant other at least twice a month. Running a business is both time and attention consuming. Fight against this trap. Allow for sufficient time and energy to be an engaged spouse, parent, and/or friend.

Define Your Life

Want more life? To change, you must change your mindset. Begin now to set a goal to work less, make more, and have more life! These are achievable goals. To be truly fulfilled, you cannot be focused solely on financial goals. Set personal goals to have more fulfillment, balance, and joy in your life. Fulfillment is an inside game. Examine your heart. Know what you truly want. According to Socrates, "The unexamined life is not worth living."

While you probably have a vision for your business, you most likely don't have one for your personal life. Without a personal vision or game plan, your personal life will always be an afterthought, haphazardly conducted, chaotic. If you fail to plan, you will plan to fail in your personal arena. Work on your life. Be proactive, not reactive.

The solution is simple, get a vision and get a life! Know who you are and what you want. Don't live your life based on the expectations of others. It's your life to live. Success is getting what you want; happiness is wanting what you get. Now is the time to stop whining and complaining. It's time to create the life you want. However, you must decide your heart's desires. No one can do this but you. You get to invent your life and set the terms and conditions. Who and what are most important to you? What do you want your personal life to look and feel like in one year, three years and five years? Once you know what you want, be true to yourself and live the life you want, not what others want.

Begin by asking many questions:

- What's most important to me in life?
- In my heart, gut, and soul, what do I truly want for my life?
- What don't I want?
- What are my deepest values (emotional states you desire most)?
- How do I want to spend my remaining time on earth?
- What activities do I want to participate in?
- What relationships are critical to a fulfilling life?
- Where is my life out of balance?
- What do I want to do with my greater freedom and personal time once I function as a strategic business owner?
- What relationships am I failing to nurture and develop?
- If I only have six months to live, what would I change? What would I focus on?

Also, never confuse things with values. For example, no one really values money itself (a "means" value). Rather, people value money for what it represents or fulfills on an emotional level (an "end" value) -- freedom, security, power, accomplishment, etc.

In my opinion, real fulfillment comes from the deep connections we make with other people and our God on an emotional and spiritual level. The answer to fulfillment is not more money or bigger and better toys. Money, new cars, houses, clothes, and jewelry will not fill in the empty holes in your soul. Only by living a life in alignment with your values (core beliefs) will you experience deep fulfillment, joy, balance, and happiness. Also, in order to avoid burnout, you must consistently make and take the time to renew and refresh your battery.

Get Help Letting Go

Giving up day-to-day control of a business is hard. Letting go of the reins can be scary. Delegating can be a challenge. However, to have more life and more fulfillment, you cannot do it all. Quit being a micro-manager or control freak. You must give up to go up. You must yield control to gain freedom.

It's physically impossible to manage every aspect of a business. You must trust your people and the planning, procedures and policies you have put in place. Reluctance to trust others and rely on them is a weakness, not a strength. Trust the integrated business system you created.

If you haven't done so (and shame on you for not taking action already), get a business coach who will help you to:
- Become a Strategic Business Owner.
- Work **on** your business instead of **in** your business.
- Focus more on tomorrow and less on today.
- Tackle important matters, not urgent matters.
- See and face reality (your repeated, external behavior) - not allowing you to rely on your internal perceptions.
- Think and act like a CEO, not a front-line employee.
- Put business systems in place to replace you.
- Lead your team and leverage your opportunities.
- Create a simple business plan.
- Set personal and business goals and keep you accountable for reaching them.

If you do not want a personal coach, ask one of your advisers to serve this critical role.

Again, if you can't keep out of the details or if you are not focusing on your areas of brilliance, think about bringing in a professional manager or executive. Consider hiring a President or Chief Operating Officer to handle the day-to-day issues of the business while you focus on the more strategic areas.

Value Your Time More Than Money

Broaden your definition of wealth. Wealth is more than just money. Real wealth is about physical and mental health, close relationships, and emotional and spiritual well being, to name a few. You can have lots of money but still be lonely and emotionally bankrupt.

Furthermore, you can always make more money, but you can't make more time. How much money do you really need? How much is enough? Time should have much more value and importance to you than money. Again, what do you want to do with your personal time? What's most important to you? To have fulfillment, you have to choose how you spend your time.

Do not confuse busyness with productivity. Don't confuse activity with accomplishment. Always ask, "What is the highest and best use of my time?" Focus on "what and why" and less on "how". Use the 80/20 rule to your advantage. What 20% of your talents, skills, experiences will give your company the greatest return? What 20% of the organization can you focus on to yield the greatest bottom-line results? You should never have to work more than 9-10 hours per day, especially after a few years in the business. If so, you are working hard but not smart. Change the mindset – long hours don't necessarily equate to success.

Stop trying to manage every second of every day. Start managing important relationships, both inside and outside the company. Focus on those individuals you need to spend time with, those that need your love, attention and mentoring. Focus on people and priorities.

Barriers to Change – Be Aware

Why do so few owners embrace new ways of running their businesses? Why such reluctance to change? In brief, here are some of the more common barriers to healthy change I have encountered:

- Many entrepreneurs are more comfortable with old problems and beliefs than with crafting new solutions. They prefer the known to the unknown. Inertia has set in. Complacency has set in.

- Some are too short sighted. They will not endure short-term sacrifice and discomfort in order to create long-term benefits. This is similar to people struggling to stop smoking, lose weight, begin exercising, etc. The avoidance of short-term pain is greater motivation than the desire for long-term pleasure and benefits.

- Owners are prisoners to their habits and frames of mind. They simply fly "by the seats of their pants" and default to what they know best. They are handcuffed by their paradigms (mental pattern for seeing their environment), technical expertise and comfort zone.

- Some owners have bought into the deadly myth that business ownership requires exceptionally long hours, tough days, and much sacrifice. While this may be necessary starting out, they should not commit themselves to a life sentence of hard time. But they do! They believe deeply the "no pain, no gain" motto and quietly and secretly suffer through the blues. There is even a prejudice that "thinking, planning, and leading" are not meaningful activities. Instead, they put on their work boots and try working even harder. They dig even deeper into the details. They get busy being busy. They "just do it". Such self-delusions bring them pain, suffering and bondage.

- Some owners are convinced that they have all the answers and are not receptive to challenging old assumptions or considering new ideas that could substantially improve their businesses and lives. They spend precious energy always defending what they know for sure. Little can be done to help these folks. They are not coachable.

- But the overwhelming barrier to change is that most owners are too busy to slow down, reflect, and set a new course. As a result, they never escape the daily "fire drills" to think about and implement better strategies. When surrounded by smoke, you cannot see the big picture and big changes that need to take place to improve your business and your life. Instead you instinctively and reactively tackle low-priority, high-urgent tasks. Use this book as your forced reflection.

You must accept that with help, you can overcome most of these barriers. In fact, consider them convenient excuses. Identify which of these barriers is your favorite excuse for not taking action. Commit to kill this excuse and overcome inertia. Engage your coach in the process.

Other Suggestions for Happiness

- Don't try to be better than others, simply try to be the best you can be.
- Don't compare yourself to others; someone will always possess something to a greater degree (money, material things, youth, looks, size of company, etc.).
- Magnify your blessings; focus on what you already have, not what you don't have.
- See life through a lens of abundance, not of scarcity; others don't have to lose for you to win.
- Live the life you want, not the life others want for you.
- Live by design, not by default.
- Stop seeking happiness in the wrong place; it is not found in things.
- Keep learning as if you were immortal, live life fully realizing that you are not.
- Don't seek visible things as much as invisible things.
- Change what you must, accept what you can't change.

Suggested Action Items:

- Realize you are not the business and the business is not you. It is a separate entity. Your value as a human being is separate from the value of your business.
- Acknowledge your mortality. When you face death, you can truly begin to live life. Remember what you want on your tombstone and live your life accordingly. Do not live according to the expectations of others – it's your life.
- If you are married or have a significant other in your life, make sure that they read this book as well. After you finish the book, give them thirty days to complete it as well. To understand you and your situation better, they need to appreciate your world and your challenges more fully.

Given a common foundation of understanding, there can be more frequent and open communication and richer collaboration. Do not try to be a silent, stoic, lone ranger anymore!

- Ask your spouse or significant other to provide you with continual feedback on your progress at home. Over time, they should sense a more relaxed, engaged, and joyful spouse, parent, and friend.

- Winning at business but losing at home is not success. A balanced and fulfilling life is success. Therefore, schedule family time each week. Plan for and spend unencumbered time with your family members throughout the week and give them your undivided time, love and attention.

- Plan and schedule two dates a month with your spouse or significant other.

- Again, insist that your spouse or significant other and key business advisers read this book. They can't help you unless they understand your challenges and the solutions.

- Get a life. Get a vision for your personal life. Similar to designing your business, design the type of life you want to live. Share this with your coach and your spouse/significant other. Know what is most important to you and shape your life accordingly.

- Use your coach to help you let go. If you can't let go and get out of the details, hire a professional business manager.

- You can always make more money, but you can't make more time. Time should have much more value and importance to you. Stop trying to manage your time. Start managing important relationships, both inside and outside the company. Focus on those individuals you need to spend time with, those who need your love, attention and mentoring.

- Before doing a task, ask, "Does this task lead directly to increased profits, significantly reduced costs, improved customer satisfaction, or to me building a better business"? If it doesn't, dismiss the task or delegate it.

- Again, do those things that only you can do as CEO and delegate the rest. You need to free up time to do CEO activities that make your business and personal vision a reality.
- Admit to yourself that you have habits, comfort zones and paradigms (mental models) that are holding you back. Set a goal to discover and confront these mental beasts. Share these barriers with your coach and spouse/significant other so they can be on the lookout. However, see these barriers as excuses that can be overcome with the strategies in this book and with the help of your accountability team.
- Choose to live a life by design, not by default!

Some Final Points to Ponder

- *Thinking is the hardest work there is. That is why so few people engage in it.*
  Henry Ford
- *It is not necessary to change. Survival is not mandatory.*
  W. Edwards Deming
- *It's what you learn after you know it all that counts.*
  John Wooden
- *The art of being wise is the art of knowing what to overlook.*
  William James
- *Plan your work for today and every day, and then work your plan.*
  Norman Vincent Peale

CONCLUSION

It's time to begin building a better business, a better you, and a better life. It's time to re-shape your thoughts and philosophies. It's time to put joy back into your life and into owning a business. It's time for you to re-acquire the fire, the passion, the excitement, and the joy of owning a business.

Yes, you can work less, earn more, and have greater freedom and joy. This book showed you how. Realize it's the mental game that matters most. Change your mental models and mental maps and you move in the right direction with far less effort and pain. Again, it's all about shifting mindsets, not shifting gears. Be open to a between-the-ears makeover. The right habits and strategies are much more important than the right tactics. This book has been about mentally adopting the right strategies and attitudes. Did you get a coach to help you transform? If not, you will not achieve optimal success and happiness. Get a coach on your side, helping you to work "on" yourself, "on" your business, "on" your life, and "on" your dreams and goals.

To refresh your memory, here is the process to greater freedom, fortune and fulfillment. The way to work less and make more. The answer to working smarter, not harder.

- **Step One:** Learn to work **on** yourself by transitioning to a new way of thinking and behaving. Re-program yourself and your habits. Stop acting like an employee and start thinking like a CEO. Learn to work **on** your business, not **in** your business. Adopt the theory of optimization. Be strategic, not tactical; work less, lead more!
- **Step Two:** Systematize your company by creating, documenting and continually improving all your key

processes, procedures and policies. Trust the business system and personnel you put in place and remove yourself from the company's daily details. Be more hands-off and more brains-on. Replace yourself with other people. Define and document the work to be done. Train others and delegate the work. This operating system is your foundation for freedom.

- **Step Three:** Increase your leadership capabilities. Excel at leadership, not doer-ship. Your business needs a clear vision and strong leader to hold others accountable, not another employee doing technical work. Help build and direct your team.
- **Step Four:** Develop clarity of direction for your business and employees by creating a simple business plan and an effective implementation process.
- **Step Five:** Learn to effectively manage your people, your greatest asset.
- **Step Six**: Instead of incremental growth, engage the leverage of marketing to achieve substantial, profitable growth.
- **Step Seven:** Learn to let go, delegate, and truly enjoy business ownership and your life.

Success is getting what you want; happiness is wanting what you get. I hope you will be both successful and happy. You are the author and architect of your business and life. You alone are responsible for designing your business life and personal life. Make sure you design them to work for you and to fulfill your desires.

If this book helped change your mindset, it was a success. The key to successful and happy business ownership is to transform your mind. You must start thinking and acting like a CEO, not an employee. If you start leading and better leveraging your time, talent, and resources, you will be happier with your business, your life, and your results.

Now, go work "on" your business and "on" your personal life.

God bless you and your business.

Daniel M Murphy

Daniel M. Murphy

"Enhancing the strategic mindset, focus and results of small business owners, franchisees, managers, and the self-employed."

Owning and running a business, done right, should be about generating significant money, freedom and fun. Are you on track? If not, please get some help.

The Growth Coach® is North America's leader in business coaching. Our professionally trained and certified business coaches are located throughout the United States and Canada. They understand deeply the philosophy, strategies, mindsets and process described briefly in this book. They are also certified in The Strategic Mindset®, a year-round coaching and accountability process that helps business owners to achieve greater focus, freedom and financial success. You can locate a business coach near you by visiting **www.TheGrowthCoach.com**.

The Strategic Mindset® Process is a proven and guaranteed strategic-focusing process. This process has been helping entrepreneurs for over a decade. Clients participate in unique personal strategic retreats one day every quarter to help achieve greater success and balance in their lives. They discover personal management and business management strategies and mindsets that are practical and highly effective. Clients get to slow down, reflect, face reality and decide on the critical changes they need to make to improve their businesses and lives. They come away from each session armed with a 90-day strategic plan, as well as greater clarity and confidence about achieving their vision, strategies and goals.

In addition to quarterly group coaching, Growth Coach® professionals can also deliver one-on-one coaching, tele-coaching, management team development, sales team coaching and special project assistance. All services come with a unique, no-hassle money-back guarantee.

To learn more, visit www.TheGrowthCoach.com.